The Karma of Everyday Life

The Karma of Everyday Life

David Lacey

BOOKS

Winchester, UK
Washington, USA

First published by iff Books, 2013
iff Books is an imprint of John Hunt Publishing Ltd., Laurel House, Station Approach,
Alresford, Hants, SO24 9JH, UK
office1@jhpbooks.net
www.johnhuntpublishing.com
www.iff-books.com

For distributor details and how to order please visit the 'Ordering' section on our website.

Text copyright: David Lacey 2012

ISBN: 978 1 78099 874 9

A CIP catalogue record for this book is available from the British Library.

Design: Stuart Davies

Printed and bound by CPI Group (UK) Ltd, Croydon, CR0 4YY

We operate a distinctive and ethical publishing philosophy in all
areas of our business, from our global network of authors to
production and worldwide distribution.

CONTENTS

For my beloved sister Jackie

Introduction

In November 1994 newspapers carried a report about an Iraqi terrorist called Khay Rahnajet, who didn't pay enough postage on a letter bomb he had made. It came back with 'Return to Sender' stamped on it. Forgetting it was the bomb, he opened it and was instantly killed.

To many folk, this is a classic example of karma. We pay for our bad deeds; we are blown up by bombs of our own making. There is no need of human intervention, no need of judgement or a court; nature somehow ensures that we get what we deserve. We each post letters to ourselves, both good and bad. They bounce around the universe and somehow end up back on our own doorstep.

Karma is an eastern word that has now entered the western lexicon. It is a vast, subtle and all-encompassing concept. It affects us all; it is one of the prime influences on our life's journey. Most people are familiar with the idea yet, paradoxically, few understand it.

But in a sense this is true of many areas of human understanding. We in fact know very little, despite our certainties and our intellectual bravado. We have taken but a spoonful from a vast mountain of knowledge. Fortunately our understanding of the natural world is increasing all the time. It seems to come to us in fits and starts. The graph of knowledge versus time appears to be a series of irregular steps rather than a smooth upward curve. A new idea is born, followed by a period of reflection, confirmation and assimilation. Each step is constructed from small mosaics, discrete bits of information that combine to form a whole. As each piece is added a larger picture begins to emerge.

An example of this is what quantum scientists call 'The Standard Model.' It is a hypothesis, an abstract theory which describes the way elementary particles behave and how the fundamental forces of nature affect those particles. The standard model is not yet fully proven, but slowly, over decades, it is being verified one step at a time, using mathematics and experimentation. It has intrigued physicists for over a century, and at the time of writing they are searching for a particle known as the Higgs Boson, which will provide one of the final and most significant pieces of the picture. The Standard Model will no longer be a theory; it will be a truth.

This seems to be how science works. This is how knowledge evolves. A new idea, a flash of imagination somewhere deep inside a scientist's brain, opens the door to a new way of looking at the natural world. Other scientists learn about it, they discuss it and eventually somebody sets about verifying it. The verification process takes place in steps. A picture begins to take shape over years, decades, even centuries, as scientists fill in the remaining gaps.

Another example of this step-by-step approach is the periodic table, which lists in rows and columns all of the chemical elements. It was first proposed by George Mendeleev in 1867, though his table had more gaps in it than elements. But it proved to be an accurate predictor of what might later be found. Chemists looked at the patterns and were able to deduce the existence of elements long before they were actually discovered. Over many decades experiments confirmed their reality, and so the hypothesis was confirmed.

Few theories arrive fully-formed and open to complete verification. Science seems to be a sort of cosmic paint-by-numbers game; the more we work at it the clearer the overall picture becomes. We start with a belief, develop a theory and then gradually fill in the blanks. On the way to completion our confidence in the truth of the theory increases, step by step.

Is there such a thing as a Standard Model for the spiritual side of life, of karma, of what some call the perennial philosophy? We have lots of disparate beliefs – which often seem at odds with each other – but is there a model that we can, step-by-step, verify and confirm, so that even though the verification will remain incomplete we can refer to it with ever increasing confidence?

If there *is* a standard model perhaps it would read something like this: We each find ourselves here on earth, vulnerable and maybe a little perplexed, and conscious of the short and brutish nature of life. We struggle for our allotted three score years and ten and then we die. But a part of us continues. We find ourselves in a different realm, a realm where thoughts predominate. The life we have just left and the way we lived it affects the situation in which we now find ourselves, a heaven or a hell that we have created for ourselves. We soon discover that the nature of this new existence is determined by the quality of our thoughts: if we are full of love then that is what we experience but if we give out hate then nature gives us that experience too.

We eventually return to this world in another body, with our circumstances largely determined by our desires, our thoughts, our karma. Gradually, over many such lifetimes, we begin to realise that there is a developmental process going on. We become slightly wiser with each lifetime and begin to recognise patterns. Our compassion grows and our values develop. We see that we are in a sort of cosmic game of snakes and ladders where we can, through our own behaviour and choices, make progress towards happiness and fulfilment. But we can also make mistakes and slide back to a lower level.

Over dozens, maybe hundreds, of these learning experiences that we call life we develop higher values and a greater under-standing. Eventually we become what some call 'enlightened' and we can, so the theory goes, choose to leave this earthly coil and pursue our spiritual growth in a different way, a way that may be beyond our current vision.

This is not a standard model that everyone would agree with, though it would in fact find a lot of common ground with

Vedanta and Theosophy, and with eastern religions such as
Hinduism, Taoism and Buddhism.

There are numerous belief systems in the world, but that is all
they are, beliefs, dogma. Belief may be defined as the act of
holding something to be true despite an absence of evidence. It
can be a starting point for a theory, but it must then move on to
something more tangible if it is to have value as knowledge. If a
belief does not lead to investigation and evidence-seeking it
eventually stagnates, a process that prevents debate and
dampens curiosity. It only has value as an emotional comforter.
This can breed the arrogant certainty of dogmatism which, as
history tells us, can so easily lead to tragedy on a massive scale.
The seeker of knowledge is one who attempts to go beyond
belief, beyond dogma, towards understanding, verification and
ultimately truth.

So can this standard model of spirituality lend itself to investigation? Can these beliefs be verified, and so become a body of
knowledge that we can have confidence in. Can we fill in some of
the blank spaces in our standard model, so that we can be sure
that we are travelling in the right direction?

So many spiritual books simply state beliefs as if they are
facts, whereas upon investigation they prove to only have the
veracity of speculation or wishful thinking. They are like poetry:
enjoyable and perhaps comforting to read but in fact only able to
offer a temporary solace. The shelves in many bookshops are
laden with volumes about spiritual issues, some of them sensible,
some of them strange and some of them quite bizarre. When I
read any of these books I often ask myself: how does the author
know this? Why does he or she expect me to accept this point of
view? Where does this certainty come from? Such books will
assert that there *is* a life after death, that there *is* a phenomenon
known as karma, and we will be asked to take the author's word
for it. No proof is offered. Thus these concepts remain beliefs and
do not mature into knowledge.

This is not enough for many of us. We are not innocent villagers in a primitive society, easily won over by the enthusiastic rantings of a witchdoctor. We need an informed viewpoint, one in which we can trust. If we are to value spiritual ideas we must have confidence that they are sensible and honest. We each have doubts and scepticism, so why should we accept an idea if we are not offered evidence to support it?

We have largely left behind the age of superstition and ignorance. We see the shortcomings of ideas that rely on blind faith, dogma or fear. We look instead for concepts that are tangible, that can be verified empirically, that have some basis in reason and logic.

And sometimes we find those ideas.

It was once my singular good fortune to enter into a long correspondence with a doctor in India. He had a vast and all-encompassing intellect. He was curious about everything and dogmatic about nothing – a wonderful combination of characteristics – and he was relentless in his search for knowledge. He frequently exhorted me to 'Seek truth, not comfort.' We saw things quite differently, which is not surprising given our disparate cultural backgrounds, but he was insistent that a synthesis of Eastern and Western knowledge would be beneficial to all of us. I consistently tried to see his point of view and I like to think he did the same with mine. What follows is a record, I hope a fairly accurate record, of our conversations.

The letters fall naturally into four sections. Firstly, we need to assess the strengths and weaknesses of human knowledge systems, especially philosophy and science, as we may easily be misled. Secondly, what exactly is karma? Can we clearly define it? What do the ancient scriptures say about it? Thirdly, how do we know that the idea of karma is true? It would be a waste of time to discuss a phenomenon if we can't in fact be sure that it exists. And finally, how does it work? How does it affect us, our circumstances, our life's journey?

An understanding of the Laws of Karma can be of benefit to each of us as individuals, and possibly to mankind as a whole. But it must be an understanding based on reason and honesty, not on fear or a desire for comfort.

Chapter 1

Indian Summer

The cottage we lived in at that time was old, isolated and in need of repair. Ivy grew around the twisted windows and the sundial was covered in moss. Some tiles on the crooked roof were cracked. One summer night there was a storm and the old apple tree was blown over. Some guttering came loose and fell to the ground. Rainwater tumbled onto the path and into the kitchen; it took us a week to clear up the mess.

We laughed at our small misfortunes and took nothing seriously. We drank wine with friends, took picnics down into the valley and invented lyrical theories about everything. Sandra played the flute and I wrote poems about Nordic gods, wild animals and colourful birds. They had names like Socrates, an oriole that sang in the evenings, and Goethe the Goat, who head-butted his way into a history lesson at the nearby school. Goethe the Goat ran for twenty-one pages; I was proud of his adventures and grew to love him. Goat rhymes with boat, stoat, moat and a myriad of delightful words that allowed him to engage in a world of excitement born of curiosity.

Sandra and I had long rambling conversations with friends about art and beauty and ethics and myths, talking until the small hours, laughing at our own pretentious wisdom. Later I would awaken and phone my office with an excuse. My colleagues regarded me as a slightly eccentric but nonetheless useful team member, so my minor transgressions were usually tolerated. In any case, I made them laugh and I brought them fruit and honey from my small orchard. I had seven bee hives at the end of the garden, under the pear trees. We called them the Seven Pillars of Wisdom. Their industrious residents produced the occasional gifts of honey that kept everyone at my office sweet.

Each August we would lie on our backs in the garden at midnight and watch for Perseid's dreams as they offered us tiny moments of illumination. 'There's one...' and it was gone. A tiny particle, the world in a grain of sand, lit up our lives for a moment, made us brighter, then magically vanished. We created images around them: 'That was Michelangelo,' Sandy exclaimed.

It seems like a happy dream now, looking back. I remember it with the fond sadness of something lost.

I worked at the time for a medium-sized engineering company. The office was six miles away; often I would cycle to work. It was downhill all the way, so I would arrive perspiration-free. The journey home was an ordeal, but by the time I reached the cottage I had worked away the contaminants of my daily routine. In fact the stresses were few and far between. I could have had more responsibility, far more. Instead I chose a life of honey, poetry and shooting stars. I had never found material things important. I possessed the small amount of intuition, or perception, call it what you will, to realise that a more challenging role would not necessarily bring me greater fulfilment. The lives of some of my colleagues seemed to bear this out. I had enough stimulation and income to keep me interested, and that was sufficient for my working life.

I was twenty-seven when I married Sandy. She was another shooting star. She arrived in my life and I was illuminated and excited. She loved my bright red braces, my round gold spectacles and my selection of crumpled flat caps. And she said she loved me. We got married three months later and moved into the tumble-down cottage I had bought a year earlier with the intention of renovating.

We liked to travel and went to many exciting places: Greece, Norway, Italy and Egypt. Then we set off for India. Sandy said we would find ourselves there; we could talk to fortune tellers, wise gurus and learned pundits. I agreed, albeit with a discreetly raised eyebrow. We searched for an astrologer at an address we had been given, in a narrow, cluttered side street in Agra, and were told he was away on a pilgrimage. So we went to see the Taj Mahal by moonlight and put the future on hold for the time being.

In Jaipur we saw the great stone astrological instruments of Jai Singh, and marvelled at the palaces. Colours rioted everywhere: the open-air spice stalls, the flowers, and the almost fluorescent yellow and red saris worn by the beautiful black-haired girls who hurried past. More than anything I loved the elephants, the camels, the street monkeys, the holy cows and the shifty-looking snake charmer with his cobra and mongoose. A wiry fellow with a turban, loin cloth and a stick strode along the street with two sad looking dancing bears. It distressed us both. The bears stared in a way that remained with us for days.

The accident, I suppose, was inevitable. I turned to cross a road, looked the wrong way and stepped out in front of a put-putting taxi. It put-putted me into a hospital. The memory of it is now hazy, but I can still hear that screech of tyres and Sandy's cry. I was taken to a clinic with a fractured wrist and mild concussion. I suppose I'd got away lightly. We wondered later if the absent astrologer could have armed us with some foresight.

I still remember the kindness of the staff at the clinic. The waiting area was crowded, and people stared at me with an open innocence. I felt embarrassed; I was placed at the front of the queue and X-rayed within a few minutes. They were all genuinely concerned; I was a visitor from afar and I needed their help.

I was checked over by Dr Ramana. He was of medium stature, about fifty years old and had an air of gentle dignity about him. I immediately trusted him – I can remember that quite clearly, even after all these years. The staff were in awe of him, I could see. They never took their eyes from him and he spoke to them with a quiet good humour. The details of my conversation with him are naturally difficult to recall after all this time, but I do remember his heavy accent and his difficulty with some English words.

I made a somewhat lame joke about my accident being caused by bad karma. He looked at me curiously. "Karma is neither good nor bad. It just is," he said with a gentle smile. "Like gravity."

For many years afterwards, Sandy and I would mimic a strong Indian accent. "Karma is neither good nor bad," I'd say. "It just is."

Sandy would laugh. "Like gravity."

My wrist was set in plaster and I was taken to a ward; I needed observation because of the concussion. Again I felt uncomfortable; everyone else seemed in a far worse state than me. I was occupying a bed under what I thought were false pretences. And in any case, the accident had been my fault.

Sandy went back to the hotel. Late in the evening a nurse gently stroked my hand to waken me; I must have dozed off. She informed me as she tidied the bed that the doctor would be coming to see me again. Dr Ramana appeared a few moments later and checked my eyes with a small torch. He then sat on the chair next to my bed and took my pulse. He closed his eyes for a full minute, then opened them and looked around the room.

He turned to me and smiled. "So," he said. "You know about Indian philosophy?"

I wish I could remember the exact details of our conversation but it is now so long ago. I told him that before studying engineering I had done a year of philosophy at university.

"Western philosophy," he corrected me, with a formal nod of his head.

The conversation lasted for about half an hour. Tired and aching though I was, I enjoyed listening to him. There was something captivating about this man. He was brilliant yet humble, without ego. He was gentle and kind, yet no-one would ever take advantage of his kindness. I felt, as he looked at me and spoke, that all of his attention, all of his compassion, was focussed upon me and me alone. He told me, in soft and accented English, that he came from a family of Brahmins and had grown up able to recite whole chapters of the Vedas. He had studied medicine at Oxford under a scholarship scheme, then done a Masters degree in Sanskrit before returning to India to become a doctor. His children had now left home, he said, and he was planning to leave the medical profession one day to devote himself to the spiritual life.

As I sit here now, many years later, it is difficult to recollect much of our talk. But at the time it made me feel somehow that all was right with the world; everything was in its proper place. My broken wrist, for example, was fine; it was all part of an unfolding of events and nothing to be concerned about. It was just a small part in a much greater cosmic plan. I remember feeling uplifted and at home, in harmony with my surroundings. I half expected my injured wrist to glow with light and spontaneously heal.

A nurse came and spoke softly to Dr Ramana. He smiled. He looked at me and raised a finger."You must sleep," he said. "Close your eyes."

He closed his own eyes and made himself at ease in his chair. I watched him in the low light. The hospital ward was quiet. In the distance I heard the diminishing clip-clop of a nurse's heels.

"Close your eyes," he said again, gently. I felt no need to move, or to make myself comfortable. My mind sank effortlessly into a white, soundless void.

I didn't hear him leave. Throughout the night I was not sure whether I was awake or asleep. I was in a strange dream-like state. I was asleep, but somehow I was aware that I was asleep. I was watching myself, silently, with an all-pervading sense of peace. And I knew, absolutely, that whatever happened I would be fine.

I didn't see Dr Ramana again, ever.

Sandy came the next day and I was discharged from the hospital. We continued our travels, albeit with more caution when crossing streets. We had fallen in love with the country, with its people, its culture, the atmosphere of history and mystery. It awakened magical memories in me, of childhood picture books of Persia, Mesopotamia and Siam, of camel trains and spice merchants, and an India where Bengal tigers roamed the misty forests.

The image that remains with me to this day is of the luminous, vibrant colours of the saris, and the sad, reproachful expression of those two dancing bears.

About a fortnight after we returned to England I sent a small donation to the hospital. I was grateful for their help and kindness; I remembered my short stay there with genuine fondness. I addressed my letter to Dr Ramana and I mentioned that I had enjoyed our conversation. I told him I hoped he would find fulfilment when he embarked on his spiritual journey. Naturally I did not keep a copy of my letter; I didn't realise I would be writing about it many years later

Dr Ramana replied about a month later. It was a neatly typed letter of about five pages, and I studied it eagerly. Sandy thought the letter amusing but unimportant. She couldn't understand my interest in it. But I found it intriguing. I still had this image in my mind of Dr Ramana sitting by my hospital bed, and the strange, dreamlike state I had succumbed to, which I somehow attributed to him. I explained this to Sandy.

"It was probably the drugs," she said. "Painkillers."

"I wasn't given any," I replied.

I read and re-read Dr Ramana's letter, and somehow thought it contained a lot more than just words. And maybe I was right. Maybe I would learn something.

Dear David,

It was extremely generous of you to send us donation so thank you

and please to be assured that it will be put to good use in the hospital and yes of course I am remembering you because we talked one evening when you were here with a concussion as we thought you may have cracked your skull from which I hope you are now fully recovered.

I am remembering our conversation very well and I reflected about it afterwards because we spoke about differences between Western and Eastern philosophy which is very interesting subject and which I later discussed with my father who is very learned (and very old!) Brahmin and like many Hindus enjoys to make specu-lation about these things even though we never reach conclusion although having said that we did in fact reach something of a conclusion in this case even though it is huge generalisation, I admit, but it is none the worse for that if you accept the limitations of a generalisation.

So we therefore decided that if we imagine a line on map of the world drawn north to south in the region of, say, Pakistan where to the left are the three religions, the Semitic religions, of the west: Judaism, Islam and Christianity and to the right of our line are the oriental religions, Hinduism, Buddhism, the Taoists, Jains and Sikhs all of which prompts us to ask where are the similarities and where are the differences?

The western beliefs to the left all have one thing in common in that they each look for their fulfilment outside of themselves and aspire to attain their rewards in far away and separate place called heaven and their God is also separational, a long way off and thus unapproachable except by good behaviour and petition.

But in the East we are introspective so the Buddhists have Nirvana, the Hindu has unity with Brahman, the Zen monk searches for Satori and they each have in common that they look within for their spiritual goal which means they turn their attention inwards and they meditate to refine their nervous system with yoga all of which is an inward-looking process although of course there are many outward manifestations such as temples, statues and so on *although these are in fact just aids to our inner journey and thus they are only valued for the benefits they bring to our consciousness.*

But this is huge generalisation or a pattern or trend seen over millions of people because when I use the term Hindu it is collective noun used to denote hundreds of millions of individuals each with their own interpretation of what Hinduism really is and some indeed will be outward-looking and same goes for westerners of whom some will be introspectionistic although I believe that this generalisation of mine does contain some water because religious art seems to confirm it as for example the classical image of Buddhist or indeed Buddha himself is one of closed eyes and the attention is turned inwards whereas early Christian paintings show worshippers turning their gaze upwards as though their God has a specific geographical location somewhere at higher physical elevation and hell, of course, is always down below.

I am always interested to learn more about these things and to understand the viewpoint of another person especially a western person who may see things differently.

Yours sincerely, K Ramana

Dr Ramana's letter was interesting and, despite its generalisations and imaginative use of words, made a valid point. Generalisations, I soon came to realise, were characteristic of his view of the world.

I have to openly admit that I am quite sceptical, even cynical, about religions in general. One cannot deny that many people get solace from their beliefs, and a lot of good things are done by people of a religious persuasion, but one can never ignore the intolerance that religions frequently breed; the idea that I am correct so you must, per se, be wrong, which leads to so much cruelty and injustice. But I knew little of eastern thought. Our recent travels had made me curious. It was clear that spirituality is an intrinsic part of day-to-day living in India, and their view of the cosmos, their paradigm, was both new to me and quite mysterious.

I replied to Dr Ramana a couple of weeks later. This time I did keep a copy.

Dear Dr Ramana

Thank you for your long and interesting letter. I found your point about East-West differences quite intriguing. There is I'm sure a divide somewhere over the Hindu Kush. I have noticed this before, but in a somewhat different way to yourself. Let me explain.

Some time ago, before I became an engineer, I studied philosophy at university. It was not a great success and I left after one year. I have to say I found much of it meaningless. Maybe I expected too much from it; I had perhaps hoped that it would reveal all sorts of profound truths, but of course it did not.

But what I noticed in retrospect was the complete dismissal of anything oriental. There was the smug assumption that 'our' philosophy was worth studying, but anything Eastern was almost beneath contempt. If someone mentioned anything to do with Eastern values he was given a tired, dismissive look. (Can you imagine physicists and mathematicians dismissing a formula simply because it was invented in the east?) I remember when one chap in a seminar mentioned déjà vu, not a particularly Eastern concept, but not 'scientifically verifiable.' and everyone rolled their eyes impatiently. We all assumed this fellow just couldn't be serious in his search for truth; he must be woolly-minded and probably wasn't tough enough to be an atheist, i.e. a proper intellectual.

My recent visit to India made me realise just how parochial our western viewpoint is. The east is a treasure-house of art, amazing architecture, intellectual attainment and all sorts of cultural gems. Westerners are often unaware of just how much the east has to offer.

The point I wish to make here is how much is lost, on both sides, by people taking a narrow view, one that excludes large proportions of the world's ideas. The east-west divide that you spoke about means that each side (it sounds like a football match, or even a war!) loses the benefit of other perspectives. How much more under-

standing could be attained by a Christian, say, or a Muslim, were he to open himself up to the ideas of looking for their God, their heaven, within themselves.

And with Western philosophers it is the same. How much more could they learn if they were not so limited and were to open their minds to different paradigms? They regard others' views as being opposed when maybe they are complimentary. But you can imagine the expressions on the faces of some very learned Oxford professors if one of their number opened up the discussion and started lecturing on, for example, reincarnation. His reputation would go up in smoke. He would no doubt receive a discreet hint from his faculty that he was damaging the university's reputation. Yet why not examine these things? They are legitimate subjects of debate.

Having said that, we must be careful not to undervalue what western thinkers have achieved. The scientific method, which began with Bacon and Descartes, has produced a working methodology that has transformed our understanding of the natural world, and yielded enormous benefits to mankind. So perhaps we shouldn't be too hard on the western viewpoint.

I hope you and your family are keeping well.

With best wishes, David

Chapter 2

Wittgenstein - The Tortured Genius

Dr Ramana replied some weeks later. For clarity I have omitted the introductory niceties with which most letters begin.

Dear David

Your letter was very interesting as it is something I have thought about a lot, and made discussion with my father especially as the philosopher who intrigues me most is your Mr Ludwig Wittgenstein, of whom I'm sure you will have read although it's not just his philosophical writings that tell the story, it is his life, as he encapsulates all that is lacking in Western philosophy.

Mr Wittgenstein defined philosophy – Western philosophy – as the logical clarification of thought and he wrote an enormously complex book (Tractatus Philosophicus) in which he tried to evaluate all our thoughts in terms of linguistic consistency and logical accuracy and the sort of precision we only find in mathematics, and I have tried to understand it, for long time I would study it for an hour each day before going to my work, but the book is self-defeating in its complexity and I suspect that in the end Mr Wittgenstein himself wasn't sure what he meant because even today professional philosophers are by no means unanimous about its value.

But the answers lie not in his book but in his life for he seems to have eventually concluded that philosophy does not achieve anything because as he says there is something inherently inadequate with the way we think about things and so to try to understand, say, moral philosophy by just piling more philosophy on top of it is simply to confuse the issue.

This mistake comes I believe from mathematics because if we want to evaluate a mathematical proposition the only tool we can use is more mathematics, but philosophy is not maths and you cannot refute philosophy with yet more philosophy because you will simply fall victim to your own argument which is in fact what happened to Mr Wittgenstein, because he wrote a whole treatise refuting a lot of human knowledge, then realised that this treatise actually refuted itself which is very funny, because he logically and positively shot himself in the foot.

Mr Wittgenstein had made one enormous error or perhaps omission is better word in that he did not turn his attention inwards, because as a Westerner he thought all the answers must be 'out there' somewhere as scientific method tells us and he thought he'd find those answers with yet more philosophy but he didn't realise he was looking in the wrong place which, as I mentioned in my previous letter, is the difference between Western and Eastern thinkers.

Since your Mr Rene Descartes, Westerners have tried to separate themselves from the object of their attention which is a process they call Cartesian Dualism and is I suppose the starting point of the scientific method which is the belief that you must be objective and separate from the object of your study, yet in some contexts this distancing of yourself is counter-productive as it creates a form of alienation.

So maybe now you can see why Mr Wittgenstein was bound to fail in his search for truth as his consciousness was distorted by fear and conflict which clouds the mind and causes poor judgement. He'd been in the trenches in The First World War, he was confused about his sexuality and he was frequently depressed so all of these issues would have prevented him from achieving clear enough state of mind to perceive truth, even if he had looked inside himself, which is what meditation does, thus allowing truth to be perceived clearly and free of the corrupting influence of the befuddlementation of the mind. If you haven't got harmony in your self, how can you ever understand harmony in music and indeed in nature, no matter how clever you are, as it is not a matter of intelligence or education but of your inner nature, your consciousness.

I wish I had met your Mr Wittgenstein. I would have said to him, "If you're so clever, why aren't you happy?"

Yours sincerely, K Ramana.

After I received Dr Ramana's letter I got a book about Wittgenstein from the library. It was called 'The Tortured Genius' and it made disturbing reading. It has to be said that poor old Ludwig had a hatful of problems. I don't know what had happened during his childhood but it must have been pretty unpleasant. Three of his brothers committed suicide; Ludwig himself contemplated it almost daily. He was depressed, anxious, obsessive and ridden with guilt. And he was cruel to children; during one spell as a teacher in an Austrian mountain village he beat a child so badly a doctor had to be called.

I was to discover two other curious facts about this unhappy thinker: he went to school with Adolf Hitler, which may explain a lot of things, and he had a brother, Paul, who was a one-armed concert pianist. You don't see many of those on a Clapham omnibus these days.

There was a strange contradiction within Ludwig Wittgenstein. His academic work was concerned with the hard-nosed rationalist material that Western philosophers love. His ideas provided the starting point for the Vienna Circle, a group of intellectuals who valued a scientific approach to philosophy and were dismissive of anything that could be termed metaphysical. They started the tradition known as Logical Positivism. But surprisingly Wittgenstein didn't apply any of this to his personal belief system, which was a naive Christianity. They were, to him, two entirely separate things. But this apparent contradiction didn't seem to trouble him; he had other things to worry about, such as walking along the pavement without stepping on the cracks, or whistling a complete piano sonata without missing a single note. And of course finding suitable ways to kill himself. It can't have been much of a life.

But perhaps we can learn something from him. Maybe we can see in his life the fact that the intellectual approach has its limitations, which are caused by our inherently inadequate way of thinking about things. And as Dr Ramana was to explain, the realisation of this can be a turning point.

Chapter 3

The Scientific Method

Dear Dr Ramana

Thank you for your interesting letter. On reflection I concluded that for you to use Wittgenstein as an example of a Western philosopher is something of a mistake; he was an extreme and atypical case, though I suppose he was useful for illustrating a point. But my main problem was with the idea of meditation as a pathway to truth. In your letter you say that meditation would perhaps provide a clearer and less confused picture of the world, but when that picture is passed on to others there is still a requirement for faith; students have to trust the subjective experience of the meditator. The student would be asked to put aside his reason and discrimination, and take things on trust. And it is that faith that I have a problem with.

Can I ask: if we cannot fully rely on the intellect, as you claim, and faith has obvious limitations, how can we ever hope to find truth? Do we use science?

Regards, David

Your question is interesting one (he replied) *and of course the scientific methodology is valuable and useful tool that as you rightly say has opened door to vast area of understanding of the natural world with medicine being just one subject which could not possibly function without the scientific method, but science, like all human knowledge, has limitations.*

The mistake many people make is to assume that this methodology can be applied to other areas of human investigation when in fact science is only applicable to small and specialised area and certainly isn't applicable to the big questions, the sort of issues that are traditionally tackled by philosophy.

For example, you often hear this sort of discussion prefaced by the phrase 'I'm a scientist....' as though that statement somehow validates what they are going to say when fact it has no relevance whatsoever because science, for all its usefulness, is an inappropriate tool for that particular dialogue.

Let me give you the example of your Mr Einstein who was once asked by a journalist if science could one day explain everything and Mr Einstein replied that he thought it was theoretically possible but it would miss the point because it would be like describing Beethoven's Ninth Symphony in terms of variations of wave pressure.

That was a good analogy because if you imagine a scientist in his white coat in a laboratory trying to establish the exact scientific nature of this wonderful piece of music he would write down every single note in terms of pitch, volume, duration, and timbre and he would end up with a pile of data one foot high on his desk and he could correctly state that this is Beethoven's masterpiece, expressed in scientific terms. But what would that pile of paper tell us? Nothing at all. It would completely miss the point, because this piece of music is an experience, it is spiritually uplifting and it is about the joy of life and the brotherhood of man, none of which can be expressed in scientific terms so for the scientist to claim that this document in any way represents the music is laughable, even though scientifically it may be absolutely accurate and correct, and reading the document will in no way convey the ideas that Beethoven was trying to express. The scientist is in fact confusing the map with the territory so to really know the Ninth Symphony and to fully understand it one must listen to it unencumbered by the intellect.

In Indian philosophy we have a concept called Pragya Parad which literally translated means 'the mistake of the intellect' and the example I have just given you illustrates the limitations of the intellect in general, and the scientific method in particular, which is not to dismiss science or indeed any intellectual pursuit, but we must recognise that there are limitations and applying science to, for example, the understanding of music is clearly a mistake. And there *are many other areas where science is not the appropriate discipline, though some scientists assume that they are qualified to pronounce on the big questions which is very much a step too far because they are simply using an inappropriate tool.*

Dr Ramana's letter makes a valid and undeniable point. It is perfectly reasonable to acknowledge that science has limitations, as indeed any form of knowledge does. No single methodology can ever cover every type of question and it is unreasonable to expect it to do so. The philosophy of science is worth considering in this context, as science is clearly a huge and vitally important area of human knowledge. It has altered the human condition immeasurably over the last century.

The scientific method is a complex subject. The word *science* is frequently misused and misunderstood. Many people, it seems to me, make a false assumption: they think that truth and scientific-ness are synonymous. They assume that if a proposition or concept has not been scientifically proven it cannot be true. This is of course nonsense. Many important propositions are true yet cannot be scientifically validated. Take for instance the statement, 'I love my dog.' You cannot scientifically verify that statement, and neither can you disprove it. You certainly cannot express it in a mathematical formula. But the statement happens to be true nonetheless. In fact many of the things that we know for certain, important things, can only be known subjectively. Science is simply the wrong tool for that particular job. And many less subjective propositions can be true, yet remain unproven scientifically. Witness statements in a murder trial may conclusively tell us the truth about a crime, but they are not scientific in themselves, even when forensic data is used to support them.

So why is the 'science' epithet so important? Probably because it bestows upon a body of knowledge a status that people will trust. For example, a government may base an expensive health programme, such as immunisation, on the scientific research that supports such a proposal. The word 'science' confers respectability and reliability. Without the reassurance of all the earlier research, such a programme would be untenable.

The theory of science goes back about a thousand years to a Middle Eastern polymath called Al-hazen, a delightful chap who devoted a lot of his time trying to prove his theory that music influenced the souls of animals. Francis Bacon and René Descartes later made significant contributions to science as did the Scottish philosopher David Hume. But the thinker of most use to us in this context is Karl Popper (1902-1994). He is generally regarded as one of the foremost philosophers in this field, and, unlike the majority of philosophers, has had a significant influence outside of his own profession, especially in the way scientists go about their business. He was scathing in his criticism of anything that smacks of scientism, by which he meant knowledge that is passed off as science when it is in fact nothing of the sort. Examples of this are Marxism, Freudian psychology and a lot of sociology.

To identify a true science Popper proposed that an idea must be susceptible to test, and thus to falsifiability, meaning that it must be theoretically possible to devise a method to refute any of the claims made within that scientific proposition. Verification of an idea, he claimed, is not enough in itself because all scientific theories are to some extent incomplete, and we can never know if and when they become complete, because we obviously do not know what discoveries may still lie in the future. Thus a scientific theory today, however valuable and correct it appears, may be contradicted or modified tomorrow by knowledge that we do not yet have. Every scientific theory is, in a sense, provisional. Because of this, verification of any theory is of limited value, as we would only ever be verifying a provisional theory. Absolute verification is, and always will be, a mirage.

Popper recognised this and proposed that the only way we

can validate a theory is to devise a way by which we can falsify it. A robust scientific theory must be one that contains elements that can theoretically be shown to be wrong. If a means of falsification cannot be devised then, ergo, the theory cannot be judged to be scientific. For this reason Freudian psychology could not be deemed a true science, because there is no way in which many of its claims can be falsified. A psychoanalyst may propose, for example, that a patient's condition B is a result of childhood event A. How could one theoretically test, and thus refute, a statement like that? How could a causal link ever be established? No experiment or observation could possibly be devised to show that such a proposition was false. Therefore it is not, in Popper's view, scientific. This does not mean however that Freud's theories are without value, or indeed untrue. They are simply not science. And dismissing an idea because it is not scientific is short-sighted, as it may in fact be very useful to us.

Clearly any proposition, scientific or otherwise, may be true or false. Attempts at verification may prove it to be false, but a theory that appears to be true must be regarded with caution, as it is in fact only a provisional truth. Even a well established concept such as Darwin's Theory of Evolution is in a sense provisional, because we do not know what information we may discover in the future that may modify it. Newtonian physics illustrates this point. The Laws of Motion were once regarded as an accurate and complete description of how moving bodies behave. But developments in quantum theory at the microscopic level, and relativity at the astronomical level, showed Newton's laws to be limited in their scope. They were not wrong; they were simply incomplete, as they applied only to a limited distance scale.

This clearly suggests that any form of dogmatic certainty is somewhat foolish. We simply do not know what we do not know.

Chapter 4

Language, Truth and Logic

A letter I wrote to Dr Ramana around this time again touched upon the question of obtaining knowledge that we can trust. If science is not adequate, I asked, what is the appropriate tool to apply to the big questions? Is it philosophy? I had my doubts, as the following excerpt from my letter shows.

The value of philosophy is a subject close to my heart; I pondered it at length many years ago. The conclusion I reached was that philosophy is a useful, indeed vital, tool of investigation, but it is unable in itself to give specific answers. Why? Because it is an algorithmic method.

An algorithm is, as you know, a term used by mathematicians and computer systems' designers to denote a deterministic procedure for deriving one form of information from another form of information. Like a game of chess, it is self-contained and does not allow influences outside of a strict set of rules. This is how computers work; to get some information out you have to first put information in, and the computer effectively re-configures it to a lesser or greater extent, according to the limiting rules of logic.

On face value philosophy can encompass any concept. We can invent, think of and debate anything we want, so it is not algorithmic. But the way we think about things is with words (we can also think in pictures and sounds but that is not relevant here). Words are in a sense not algorithmic as we can, and frequently do, invent new words to encapsulate new concepts.

But words – language – require consensus. Each and every word has an agreed meaning. There is a common lexicon that we use, and it is obviously finite. And once we step outside of that lexicon communication becomes impossible. If I say, 'Splodge is nadgely' you will not know what I am talking about. As soon as I define Splodge as my cousin's nickname and tell you that nadgely is family shorthand for angry, the sentence has meaning. To communicate, indeed to think, we have to stay within the narrowly defined confines of the common lexicon. And that turns language into an algorithmic system.

Once we are within an algorithmic system our thinking becomes restricted. It becomes like a game of chess; only certain moves and positions are available. We can only get out what we put in. We just go around and around. So philosophy becomes impotent simply because it has to rely on words. This may be why, after thousands of years of trying, there are very few, if any, certainties in philosophy; the limitations placed upon it by language means there are no definitive outcomes.

In fact this very discussion, the previous four paragraphs, illustrates this point; it is only made possible by the availability of the word 'algorithm.' Without it we would not have been able to communicate these linguistic limitations. So this in itself shows how arguments and propositions are both conditional upon, and limited by, language.

Dr Ramana replied:

Philosophy, both Western and Eastern, has serious limitations as you rightly say, but I see this problem from a purely practical point of view, which I will explain, because it seems to me that there is a polarity of ideas whenever we discuss the big questions, such as the belief in a God or an afterlife or such subjects as those.

At one extreme we have the believers and the evangelists and at the other extreme are the atheists and rationalists, and the believers have a view of the world, a paradigm, based on the idea that if you believe something it must therefore be true, and so they have an Augustinian faith, which is not a view that I can share as to me there can be no sensible connection between a believed idea and that idea existing in reality, so for example if we go down that path your Father Christmas must exist simply because lots of children believe he does. At the other end of the spectrum are the atheists and ratio-nalists who are always immensely proud of their atheism and so we have two polar opposites, the believers on one side and the atheists on the other with both sides expressing a dogged certainty. They each adopt a position then they argue FROM that position, rather than TO an outcome, and so manage to hang on to their certainty come what may.

The mediator in this dialogue is philosophy and I have very specific concern with philosophy which is simply stated: philosophy has never, and will never, yield any definitive answers. Philosophers have been debating these big issues for at least 3000 years now, since the time of Socrates indeed earlier, yet today in 21st century not one clear answer has been found, so philosophy tells us nothing and so there is simply no point whatsoever in discussing the usefulness, the validity or otherwise of these philosophical positions because no answer will ever be forthcoming.

In the last three millennia enormous progress has been made in every field of human knowledge: medicine, travel, technology, science, in fact any subject you care to name, there has been a staggering progress, yet western philosophers are still going around and around in circle, still debating the same old questions in the same old way and are no nearer to any answers than they were in Plato's time and they are in fact more confused as I illustrated with Wittgenstein.

Good example of this is radio program that is popular here in India, where six very learned guests are asked to debate a current ethical issue and this program has been broadcast for at least 10 years yet not once has the panel come up with definitive answer and each guest goes home with exactly same viewpoint with which they arrive, so even though program sounds impressive and all the arguments appear convincing it does not in fact help us out of our philosophical maze.

I will make specific prediction: over next 3000 years philoso-phers, intellectuals and theologians will continue to discuss these matters earnestly, ad nauseum but they will not, ever, come up with definitive answer to any of the big questions because philosophical discussions simply do not help us; it is not the right tool for the job and it is, once again, pragya parad, the mistake of the intellect.

This may seem an extravagant claim because after all, there are thousands of philosophers, in hundreds of universities, all writing, teaching and thinking, so who am I as outsider to make such a claim? Some may suggest that this claim cannot be made by anyone without a comprehensive and detailed knowledge of philosophy but simple analogy will show this to be untrue.

Supposing my car fails to start and I take it to repair workshop where they begin to look for fault, then I return to collect the car and the mechanic tells me that they haven't been able to find the fault and so I return next day only to be met with the same story, then I return week later and they are still discussing my car but still they haven't found solution.

The nature of this problem has now changed because the issue is no longer, What is wrong with my car? Instead it is, What is wrong with this workshop? But the important point is that for me to recognize this new problem I do not need to know specific details about cars and I do not need to be a mechanic and I do not need to understand engines to recognize that something is not right but I simply observe that no solutions are forthcoming.

Similarly with philosophy: I do not need to be an expert on Aristotle or Kant to recognize that there is something fundamen-tally wrong with this method. Why? Because, like the car workshop, no results are forthcoming and they haven't been after 3000 years of trying so there must be something wrong with the methodology. Maybe, as you say, it is due to the algorithmic nature of language.

Is there a God? Do we have free will? Is there life after death? Don't ask a philosopher, for they are simply unable to tell you and if you do not believe me find a philosopher and ask him if there is a

God and he will hop from one foot to the other and look away into the far distance.

I couldn't argue with Dr Ramana's reasoning. But it did seem a radical notion to put forward. Are all these academics and thinkers simply wasting their time? And Dr Ramana seemed to overlook the fact that studying philosophy can benefit everyone in their ability to reason and to analyse an argument. I certainly benefited from my short time as a philosophy student; I became much more incisive and perceptive about the written word.

So is all of philosophy just hot air? Everything we rely on, our religions, our political ideals, our ethical framework, the law, is somehow based on philosophy. Yet Dr Ramana has a valid point: we cannot find any certainties within philosophy whatsoever. Consider all the issues we face, such as euthanasia, abortion, free-will, consciousness; there are as many opinions as there are people holding them, which only serves to prove that there are no absolutes. More or less any argument can be proposed, and then another argument can be formulated to knock it down. Barristers use this method all the time and earn a lot of money from it; truth is almost a by-product. And so one must reluctantly conclude that the Western philosophical method is not of much use to us.

Chapter 5

Empiricism

I found myself one day leafing through Dr Ramana's letters. It was four months since we had last exchanged ideas. We had talked about many things in the last few years, but his most recent correspondence had once again touched on the impotence of philosophy. It was a notion that slightly disturbed me; without philosophy how do we get to truth? I wrote and asked him.

Dear Dr Ramana

Your letters on the subject of Western Philosophy have, I must admit, left me somewhat perplexed. I cannot dispute your logic but nonetheless I look around and see that philosophy is everywhere. Our health service, which everyone values, is in a sense altruism put into practice, and altruism is a value that we have arrived at by philosophical dialogue. We abolished the death penalty as a result of philosophical debate. Indeed our whole social structure, our democracy, is based on open and free discussion, again a form of philosophy.

You seem to be saying that we cannot rely on science, we cannot trust belief, and now we cannot use philosophy. So how do we establish truth?

Empiricism... he replied a few weeks later, *...by which I mean observation and evidence, as it is the only solid, reliable and foolproof way of securing knowledge. Empiricism, the beloved method of courts of law, of scientists, police investigators, engineers and astronomers, and sensible people the world over.*

This immediately struck a chord with me. Empiricism has an obvious appeal; it is in fact the bedrock of engineering. If your newly-designed helicopter won't leave the ground, or if your ship doesn't float, no amount of public relations spin, no advertising, no barrister's speech, no persuasion, no political posturing, no convoluted philosophy and no lame rationalisation will help you. Engineers live with one undeniable fact: you cannot argue with the laws of physics. Hence there is a delicious and unswerving honesty about engineering, which is why I chose it over philosophy.

But my immediate question was, how can you apply empiricism to an idea such as life after death? As if he'd anticipated my response, his letter went on...

Take for example the question of reincarnation, which has until recently been purely matter of faith and some people believed it, some people didn't and many people debated it philosophically, but as we have discussed they can talk about it for ever and they will not come to conclusion.

However in the last decade everything has changed because there is now a whole new way of looking at these issues and the debate is having light, indeed very powerful light, shined on it from surprising yet invaluable body of professionals: psychiatrists and neurophysiologists, who are people we can respect for their professionalism, their understanding, their academic standing and their open-mindedness. I am talking about people like Dr Raymond Moody and especially Dr Ian Stephenson, who is remarkable man.

It sounds extraordinary claim to make, but this man has single-handedly confirmed the existence of life after death to such degree of certainty that only an unreasonable person could doubt it, and the other doctor, Raymond Moody, has done similar thing in that he raised awareness of these issues throughout the world in different way but Dr Stevenson's work in particular is thoroughly objective and empirical, and is recognised as being above reproach when it comes to methodology because peer reviews have been unable to invalidate any aspect of it.

So an empirical view is now possible because of this knowledge so to return to car mechanic example in earlier letter if the mechanic looks directly at car and identifies the malfunction empirically instead of by discussion he can give proper solution to the problem so with question of life after death we can consider it empirically and establish truth without resorting to argument or belief.

I was intrigued by this new and unfamiliar knowledge. I soon obtained a book by Dr Stevenson and it opened up a new way of looking at these issues. Dr Ramana was absolutely right in his assessment of Dr Stevenson's impact on intellectual life; it was a hammer blow to the old paradigm. No longer did we have to reason, debate or believe. Here was a solid and reliable body of evidence that took the subject of life after death by the scruff of the neck.

Some decades ago Dr Stevenson, a Canadian professor of psychiatry, became aware of a number of children who between the ages of about three and seven years old would describe a previous existence, an earlier life. When he investigated these children he found that they could describe aspects of that life with such accuracy and detail that their actual identity could be established. They gave descriptions of their family, house, relatives, pets, schools, events, illnesses and much more. They were often able to describe how they had died at the end of that life.

Dr Stevenson realised that much of this information was verifiable to a very high standard. For example a child might describe how they had died, the circumstances, the cause, the hospital, the name of their doctor and so on. This data can be corroborated by, for example, death certificates, autopsy reports, hospital records, doctor's records and police accident reports, all of which had been written many years earlier. In a lot of cases family and relatives would still be alive and could confirm this information. Often a child would be taken to see his or her previous family and would be able to identify their siblings, cousins and friends. They would relate facts and nicknames that could only be known to the close family, and they could describe events in the family history, such as the death of a pet, all of which could be verified. The children themselves at that age were obviously too innocent and unsophisticated to mislead the investigators.

Dr Stevenson courageously put his professional reputation on the line to investigate this phenomenon. He devoted himself to this task for decades and travelled the world many times over. His research was hallmarked by the very highest standards of scientific rigour and integrity. By the end of his life he had compiled dossiers on over 2000 cases, each of which had dozens of facts that could be independently verified. Even his sternest critics could not doubt the validity or thoroughness of his work.

The evidence in favour of reincarnation, as delineated by Dr Stevenson, is overwhelming. His studies are scrupulously objective and methodologically impeccable. The late Herbert S. Ripley, former chairman of the Psychiatry Department at the University of Washington in Seattle, noted, "We are lucky to have someone of his ability and high integrity investigating this controversial area."

Scientists, it seems, have been unsure of how to deal with Dr Stevenson and his evidence. Many of them simply chose to ignore it as it threw doubt on their existing paradigm. But one or two recognised that this was a whole new way of looking at things. For example it has had an impact on the way psychologists interpret human behaviour. Years ago it was purely a dialogue between nature and nurture. Simply put, the nature argument was that our characteristics were defined biologically and the nurture argument held that we are the products of our environment, whether our social circumstances or our early childhood development. Suddenly there was a huge new elephant in the room. If we can somehow bring with us information from a previous life, what influence would that information exert on our current life?

What Dr Stevenson did most of all was to prove beyond reasonable doubt that consciousness is not solely a product of brain activity. It is separate from the brain and somehow our thoughts continue after death. How this happens is simply not understood, but that doesn't mean it doesn't happen.

Dr Ramana also mentioned another author in his letter, who proposed serious arguments to support the idea of a continuance of consciousness after death. In 1975 Dr Raymond Moody M.D. Ph.D., wrote a groundbreaking book called 'Life After Life'. This was the first work to deal with the topic of Near Death Experiences (NDEs) and has sold over 13 million copies.

Some years earlier Dr Moody was giving a lecture and he mentioned a phenomenon that he had come across in his medical work. He described how some patients who had technically died during a medical procedure and were then resuscitated later told of strange but reassuring experiences. Typically they would find themselves looking down on the medical team from above, watching the resuscitation process and clearly seeing the activities of the staff. Some patients told of a distant light that was somehow spiritually comforting. Others told of meeting friends and relatives who had died at an earlier time. A common experience is a panoramic life review, where they saw in fine detail the life they had led and the effect their behaviour had exerted on others. They were often assisted in this review by what they often referred to as a being of light, a spiritual figure who radiates a profound sense of peace and compassion. This being of light invariably asks one fundamental question: have you learned to love. This simple enquiry overrides all other considerations in our life, so wealth, status, fame and appearance all become insignificant. The pain that a person has inflicted upon others is now seen clearly but non-judgementally and the kindness and love that they have given are valued. The NDE was invariably a life-changing experience; people typically became kinder and less selfish afterwards.

Following this lecture Dr Moody was inundated by calls from people claiming to have had similar experiences. He embarked on a detailed study of these phenomena and interviewed thousands of people. All of this is recorded in his book. 'Life After Life' was a pioneering work which gave us a new and unique insight into the process of dying. It triggered a lot of further research by other doctors. Much valuable work has since been done by Dr Melvin Morse, Dr Elizabeth Kubla Ross, Dr Kenneth Ring and Dr Peter Fenwick.

The value in Dr Moody's work lies in its ground-breaking nature; it was the first book to look specifically at this phenomenon. But it is largely anecdotal, so perhaps does not reach the highest levels of scientific rigour. Dr Moody challenged the scientific and medical community to investigate NDEs further; he was confident that the results would validate his findings. Dr Melvin Morse, Associate Professor of Paediatrics at The University of Washington, took up the challenge. He conducted a study at the Children's Hospital in Seattle which involved a detailed review of 26 children who claimed to have experienced an NDE. Children provide a useful and relevant source of knowledge as they are innocent in their descriptions and not conditioned by social or religious mores.

Dr Morse and his colleagues compared the descriptions of NDEs with those of a carefully matched control group of 176 seriously ill children who had not died. He found that nearly all of the clinically dead patients described elements of the NDE, whereas none of the control group did, despite being in very similar circumstances. He thus demonstrated that NDEs are not fantasies caused by the resuscitation procedures and showed that just thinking you are going to die does not trigger an NDE. Later work by Dr Morse describes how the lives of people who had undergone an NDE were transformed. For example, they invariably had very little fear of dying, they were usually kinder and more spiritual (as distinct from religious) and felt that their life had a definite purpose.

However, there are always two sides to a coin. Some critics claimed that the images of a distant light or the faces of relatives were the product of the chemical changes that take place in a person's brain as they die, i.e. they were hallucinations. This has largely been disproven by further research. The consensus now is that NDEs are legitimate evidence that consciousness continues after death. The hallucination hypothesis doesn't in fact make sense. Hallucinations are by definition random; they are caused by haphazard activity in the brain. If thousands, indeed millions, of people all have the same vision then it simply cannot be judged a hallucination; there must be some process taking place that is common to all the experiencers.

Dear Dr Ramana

Your letter regarding Dr Stevenson and Dr Moody were, to put it mildly, interesting and informative. I had not realised that this sort of research was taking place and I must admit it has opened up for me a different way of looking at things. Since receiving your letter I have carried out some investigations of my own. I have discovered another doctor (I'm sure there are many more) who has an equally valid, though slightly different, point of view on these matters. You may already have heard of him, but if not I can recommend him. He is Dr Brian Weiss, and he has an interesting perspective on the reincarnation issue, born of his experiences with his patients.

(Dr Weiss is a respected psychiatrist and academic. He was educated at Yale Medical School and was Chairman of Psychiatry at the Mount Sinai Medical Centre in Miami. He has published over 37 scientific papers and book chapters in the field of psychopharmacology).

Whilst working as a psychotherapist in a major hospital Dr Weiss began treating a patient called Catherine. Her life was burdened with fear and anxiety. She feared water, choking and darkness, and she was terrified of dying. She suffered from insomnia and nightmares and her life was chaotic. Dr Weiss used hypnotherapy as part of the treatment; he took her back to her early years and they discussed events in her childhood. Then, during one particular session, Dr Weiss instructed her to "...go back to the time from which your symptoms arise." To his surprise she seemed to go back to a previous life. She was able to identify the events in that lifetime that had led to her current fears. She was able to accurately describe her life of hundreds of years ago, and the traumas that triggered her phobias. She shocked Dr Weiss by accurately revealing information about his family history, including the death of his infant son.

Dr Weiss was convinced of the validity of this knowledge. The reason was simple: as Catherine uncovered and resolved the frightening experiences from a previous life, so the symptoms that affected her in this life disappeared, just as a conventional therapist would expect had those same events occurred in childhood. During trance states she recalled past life memories which proved to be the causative factors of her symptoms. In just a few months her phobias began to disappear and she was able to live her life without the anxiety and fear. To Dr Weiss this change was proof that she had indeed suffered those traumatic events in a previous life. He went on to uncover many other cases suggestive of reincarnation and he consistently replicated the experiences hundreds of times during the following years.

I assume that these books are readily available in India, but if you have trouble obtaining them please let me know.

With best wishes, David

These three doctors, each of them respected experts in their fields, provide us with very sound evidence that consciousness continues after death. In fact the evidence is so solid and abundant that it is now irrational to dismiss the idea of a life after this one. Many other respected professionals have since corroborated, enhanced and added to this knowledge.

Put very simply, when we die we carry on thinking. How this happens and the mechanisms that allow it to take place, are not understood. How, for example, does thought occur when the complex processes within the brain are apparently not taking place? And how does information obtained in one life become transferred to another? This presents the scientific world with serious difficulties which are not likely to be resolved any time soon.

Dr Stevenson's thoroughly empirical approach may seem the most sound and reliable, but Dr Moody's descriptions of NDEs are perhaps more useful to us. He remarks on the sheer sincerity and depth of feeling on the part of people describing their experiences to him. They invariably lose all fear of death and often undergo a spiritual transformation. One person stated that he had clearly realised during his NDE that there is a simple and definite purpose to our life here on Earth. It is simply this: to learn to love one another.

This is, to me, one of the most important statements in all of history.

Chapter 6

Karma – We Are What We Think

I wrote to Dr Ramana again some weeks later asking him about the concept of karma. Karma was a word I was casually familiar with and I saw that it was invariably associated with reincarnation. Now that the truth of reincarnation had been reasonably established, I wished to learn more about this complementary idea.

I was aware that karma was an important part of eastern thought, and that it was often referred to as the law of cause and effect. I wanted to know if it was simply a part of a belief system, an idea that required faith, or could the truth of it be established empirically.

Dr Ramana replied a few weeks later.

Dear David

Of course there is karma! It is not a belief; it is descriptive noun (I'm not sure what a descriptive noun is, but no matter) *that is used to describe the action, the outcome, the result of our thoughts so it is not an abstract concept because we see it all around us all the time, for example in a building that has been designed by an architect, that is karma, it is the outward manifestation of that person's thoughts, desires, intentions.*

We see person who works hard and eventually becomes wealthy; that success is his karma, it is the tangible expression of his way of thinking, it is simply thoughts expressed in action, or desires and intentions that have come to fruition, and similarly we see lazy person and their outward life also display the tendencies of their thought patterns so once again it is empirical issue, not one arrived at by discussion or belief, because we can directly observe the effects.

Yours sincerely, K Ramana.

The following is an excerpt from my reply.

I was surprised by the down-to-earth nature of your description of karma; there was for example no reference to reincarnation. It seems to be a very simple concept, the way you describe it. I had always considered karma to be a complex and somewhat esoteric law, remote and transcendent, whereby we somehow get punished for the wrongs we have committed in an earlier time, or indeed get rewarded. I had assumed it was of a highly deterministic nature and was an intrinsic part of an overall spiritual paradigm, closely associated with reincarnation.

Dr Ramana, who comes from the Hindu tradition, surprised me with his reply by using a picture of karma neatly expressed in a quote from Buddhism. Again I have omitted the preamble. He said:

The first verse of The Dhammapada illustrates this point very clearly:

"We are what we think. All that we are arises with our thoughts. With our thoughts we make the world. Speak or act with an impure mind and trouble will follow you as the wheel follows the ox that draws the cart.

We are what we think. All that we are arises with our thoughts. With our thoughts we make the world. Speak or act with a pure mind and happiness will follow you as your shadow, unshakable."

Buddha talks about our thoughts and how they create the world in which we live, but notice that he is not saying that our actions cause our karma, just our thoughts because the actions that we take are themselves outcomes of thought and are not causes. Actions, good or bad, are the manifestation of our thoughts so if we have for example malicious thoughts which lead us to commit crime it is those thoughts that will create the negative influence in the future not the crime itself so there is no causal relationship between the crime itself and the karmic outcome; both are caused by the thoughts.

So, you may ask, if I have malicious thoughts but do not act upon them, will I still create a karmic debt for myself? Probably not, as the fact that you didn't act upon those thoughts indicates that they were not very strong or influential – they were just daydreams of somewhat negative nature but if you were to act on them and actually commit the crime, that would indicate that the malice was at a deeper more intense level, so you would commit the crime then later reap the result of having had those malicious thoughts, thus it is the intensity of the thoughts that creates the karma, not the crime itself.

This was a new and interesting way of looking at the issue of karma, and was much more acceptable, to me at least, than a karma that is a remote, deterministic law imposed on us by an outside agency. Our thought patterns, whether conscious or unconscious, clearly do influence our lives; that much seems obvious to me. So the quality of those thoughts must to some extent determine our circumstances.

A good example of thoughts in action is the work of an artist. From his innermost being an artist creates, let's say, a landscape. That landscape will somehow reflect the essence of the artist. The artist has ideas and concepts, and he translates them into the brushstrokes that appear on the canvas. That activity results in a painting. The painting is, in a way, the artist's karma; it is the outcome of his inner mental processes. It will somehow represent the thoughts of the artist, insofar as his talent will allow. It is the outward manifestation of the artist's mental processes.

According to Dr Ramana's theory, indeed Buddha's theory, we are each, with our thoughts, creating our own landscape. It is the landscape of our life. It is our karma. Our world is a reflection of our inner thoughts, our inner conflicts, our inner needs. An artist filled with mental turmoil will often produce a work that expresses that turmoil. Van Gogh is the classic example; we can clearly see this in his work. Even a simple pastoral scene is filled with the anguish and loneliness brought about by his mental illness.

John Constable's circumstances also illustrate this point. During most of his life he was a contented and fairly balanced person and he produced beautiful yet uncomplicated landscapes. Then his sister died. From then on his paintings exhibited a sense of brooding and foreboding. Dark clouds dominated the skies. These paintings represented his current state of mind; they were manifestations of his inner being.

Another example is to compare the works of the composer Antonin Dvorak with, let's say, Gustav Mahler. Dvorak was a cheerful, positive character who loved railways, pigeons and the countryside. He also loved beer, and the more beer he consumed the more he loved railways, pigeons and the countryside. He was an uncomplicated 'bloke' who apparently got on well with most people. And his music expresses this; it is always happy, melodious and uplifting.

Mahler was totally different. He was a deeply troubled man and was involved in numerous conflicts with the people around him. He lived a life of anxiety and fear; he was terrified of death. All of this can be quite clearly heard in his music; it is depressing and pessimistic, and portrays a view of the world that is unhealthy and unhappy. The title of one of his major works, 'Songs on the Death of Children', speaks for itself.

Dvorak and Mahler had similar degrees of talent but they each used it in a way that was characteristic of themselves. They expressed two entirely different perspectives. We can see this quite clearly with artists and musicians because their life is devoted to expressing their emotions and their view of reality. Their work is an outward manifestation of an inner pathology. (These examples are simply intended to illustrate a point; they are not meant to explain the psychology of art. There are many examples in history that contradict the above view. Beethoven, for instance, was renowned for being an irascible character yet he wrote some sublime and gentle music. All analogies have limits).

We can see this process working within each of us. We are all engaged in writing our own symphony. We call it 'Our Life.' We are all artists and musicians in a sense, and the life we end up with, our landscape or our symphony, is created by our own innermost state of mind. This landscape, this symphony, this life, is our karma.

We often see this with people around us. You sometimes meet somebody who is confrontational or troublesome and has difficulty getting on with people. As their life goes on and they create more and more karma so their life, their work, their health and their family situation reflects this. They may end up with family members who are alienated and angry, they may fall out with friends, or be unsuccessful at work. They find little fulfilment in life. Invariably their health will suffer.

We see on the streets of any city the sad panorama of the lives of confused and aimless people. They find themselves sleeping in alleyways and shop doorways. What puts them in this situation is, ultimately, their state of mind. They invariably have mental health issues, such as repressed anger or an unconscious fear of rejection, which lead to severe setbacks, disappointments and ill health. Research shows that homeless people are likely to die 30 years earlier than average, a third of these deaths being due to drug and alcohol abuse. They are 9 times more likely to commit suicide and 3 times more likely to die in traffic accidents. So the landscape they are creating for themselves, their karma, is one of loneliness, poverty, discomfort and ill-health. It is a reflection of their inner being.

We also see happy positive people and we can see the landscape they have created for themselves. They may have many friends and people who love them, they have security and peace of mind. They often attribute this satisfactory way of life to hard work and regular pension contributions, but those factors are results, not causes. The cause, ultimately, is their positive state of mind. The outcome, that is the satisfactory career, the sense of responsibility, and their happy and loving nature, are the result of this inner stability and strength. The life they build for themselves over many years blossoms to reflect their inner stress-free state.

How do we know all this to be true? The evidence is all around us. Talk to a homeless person and you will hear a sad tale of confusion, hurt, childhood neglect, minimal trust and low self-esteem, all of which leads to a history of poor decision making or what some psychologists refer to as 'cognitive dissonance.' A happy person will be relatively free of inner issues and thus free of conflict. This is, it must be said, a simplistic generalisation, but most psychotherapists would recognise it in their clients.

Physical health issues may also be an outward manifestation of our deeper self; they are, in a sense, the ultimate expression of our inner being. The body is continually renewing itself, shedding old material and steadily replacing its component parts. What you are today is not the same physical collection of bits and pieces that made up the 'you' of a few months ago. Everything is being regenerated continually, sometimes rapidly, like your digestive organs, which replace themselves in a matter of weeks, and sometimes over years, such as your bones. As an old Indian proverb puts it: 'You cannot step into the same river twice.' It may appear to be the same river, but it is continually changing and being renewed. Our bodies are similar; they can be seen as a process rather than a fixed collection of parts. Our quality of consciousness obviously has an impact on the way this regenerative process takes place; this is clear from our under-standing of psychosomatic illnesses. And we sometimes see examples of it in everyday life: an angry person may have an angry facial appearance. He probably has an angry liver too.

This idea seems to be borne out by academic studies. Research carried out by University College London and

Edinburgh University, published in the British Medical Journal in 2012, looked at premature deaths from conditions such as cancer and heart disease in 68,000 people, over a ten year period. Results indicated that even low levels of mental distress increase the risk by 16%. More serious problems increase it by up to 67%.

In 2011 the Cambridge Study in Delinquent Development, produced by researchers in universities in Wales and Texas, looked at data on 400 men who had originated in South London. It was discovered that in their teens and early twenties those who had criminal convictions were as healthy, indeed often healthier, than their peers. But by the age of 48 the offenders were 13 times more likely to be disabled than the non-offenders. They were also 4 times more likely to have been hospitalised in the previous 5 years.

This seems to validate Dr Ramana's concept of karma. The criminal convictions of the early years are a clear indication that something was amiss with those individuals on a psychological level. The disabilities and ill health followed later; they were the long term effects of decades of that same negative thinking. Someone who habitually offends clearly has issues at a deep level in their mind; they are simply not in harmony with themselves or with the world around them. These issues produced the criminal tendencies early on and, over the longer term, they manifested as health problems. The criminal behaviour and the ill-health were both outcomes. One did not cause the other; it was the landscape that these men had created for themselves by years of wrong-thinking.

As Dr Ramana says, karma is a law of nature, like gravity or the law of action and reaction, or indeed any of the laws of physics. There is no judgement and there is no judge. It is neither right nor wrong, good nor bad. There is no outside agency inflicting penalties or rewards.

People simply get what they ask for, as a result of their thoughts.

Chapter 7

Reincarnation – The Evidence

Dear Dr Ramana,

I am enclosing a scientific paper I have discovered written by Dr Ian Stevenson, who you referred to in an earlier letter. I am sure you will find it intriguing, as indeed I did.

You are no doubt familiar with a lot of Dr Stevenson's work, but this part is, I think, of particular interest. Whilst researching a number of cases Dr Stevenson had come to the conclusion that not just memories are transferred from one life to the next, but physical characteristics too. He realised that birthmarks on children often indicate the location of wounds inflicted during a previous life. One young man, for example, had a dozen small round birthmarks in the centre of his chest. On checking the autopsy reports of the person he had been in a previous life it was found that these birthmarks coincided exactly with the shotgun wounds that killed him.

In another remarkable case a person in a previous life was killed by a rifle bullet that entered his body and came out the other side. This was clearly noted in the autopsy and police reports. In his current life the person had two distinct birthmarks that tallied exactly with the location of the two bullet wounds. The exit wound, which was recorded on the autopsy report as being larger than the entry wound, manifested as a birthmark of greater size than the entry site birthmark. This is consistent with this type of wound, as the bullet is usually spinning on exit, so causes more damage. Dr Stevenson calculated the probability of this happening by chance. He drew on a sheet of paper the area of this man's skin as if it had been peeled off and laid flat, like taking the label from a food can. He then divided the shape into small squares and drew in the two wound sites. From this he could calculate that the probability of this being a chance event was 25,600 to 1.

These birthmarks are in a sense information that has somehow been transferred from one life to another. How that happens is simply not understood. But these are tangible pieces of evidence and they are open to empirical verification, so cannot be ignored. I would be interested to hear your ideas as to how this information is transmitted to a new life.

Best wishes, David.

The scientific paper I referred to is entitled *Birthmarks & Birth Defects Corresponding to Wounds on Deceased Persons (June 1992)* by Dr Ian Stevenson, Head of Department of Psychiatric Medicine at the University of Virginia School of Medicine, USA. Its importance and relevance suggests it deserves to be examined here in some detail.

Dr Stevenson begins the paper by stating that little is known about why birthmarks are found in one location on the body and not another. Of 895 children who had claimed to recall previous lives, birth defects or birthmarks in 313 of them could be attributed to events in a previous life. Dr Stevenson and his colleagues investigated 210 of these cases.

The paper goes on to say that such a child begins to describe the earlier life almost as soon as he or she has an adequate grasp of language, usually between two and three years of age, and ceases such descriptions at around five to seven years of age. While some of these children make only vague statements about an earlier life, others provide details that allow identification of a specific individual in that previous life. Birthmarks on such children are described as 'puckered and scarlike.' They are depressed below the surrounding area, are sometimes hairless, and with lower levels of pigmentation.

Dr Stevenson's investigations typically included interviews with the child and relatives, and the examination of all written records, such as death certificates and post mortem reports. He was careful to exclude cases where there were known causes of birth defects, such as viral infections and parental alcohol consumption.

Where a birthmark on a child's body was found to be within 10cm of the wound site in the earlier life, this was judged to be a satisfactory correspondence. An official historical document, such as a post mortem report, was available in 49 cases and corroborated the evidence. In 88% of the cases reviewed a satisfactory correspondence between the wound and the birthmark was established. This figure increased the confidence in the accuracy of other cases where no medical documentation was found.

An example is given of an Indian youth called Maha Ram. He had a hyperpigmented macule on his chest and these are shown on a photograph included in the paper. Mr Ram remembered the earlier life of a man who was killed with a shotgun. A diagram contained in the autopsy report of the deceased man showed wounds that corresponded accurately with the marks on Maha Ram's chest.

In a remarkable case a Burmese girl was born with no lower right leg. She clearly remembered an earlier life as a woman who was run over by a train and lost her leg. One unfortunate Indian boy was born with an absence of fingers (brachydactyly) on his right hand. He recalled the life of a boy who had lost his fingers in a chopping machine. Other interesting and relevant examples are included.

The paper goes on to discuss instances where there are two or more birthmarks, because in such cases the likelihood of chance accounting for the correspondence is significantly reduced. A description is given of a Thai man who recalled being killed previously by a blow to the back of the head and now had a major skin abnormality in the same location. He also had a deformed toenail, which corresponded to a chronic infection in that area in the previous life.

Eighteen cases are discussed where there are two birthmarks

which correspond to previous gunshot wounds, the bullet entering one part of the body and exiting by another. In 14 of these cases there was a correspondence at both locations. Also, the exit wound was noticeably larger than the entry wound, which is usually the case in these types of incidents.

Dr Stevenson calculated the odds against this correspondence being a matter of chance. The surface area of an average adult male is 1.6 meters, thus 160 squares of 10 cms (the distance judged to indicate a correspondence) would fit into this area. Thus, when comparing the birthmark location with that of the wound location, the probability of one position corresponding to another would be 1 in 160. The probability of two correspondences would be 1 in 160 x 160 = 25,600.

Dr Stevenson concludes with a detailed discussion of counter arguments and objections to his findings and he carefully examines other explanations. He closes by saying that he recognises the limitations of a short paper like this. It is not his intention, he says, to impose an interpretation upon the readers of his paper, but to stimulate people to examine his more detailed reports.

I found this paper fascinating. The concepts are meticulously researched and clearly communicated. It was presented to The Society for Scientific Exploration at Princeton University in June 1992.

The only aspect that I would question was the decision to use a square of 10cm x 10cm as the criteria for a valid correspondence between wound site and birthmark. This was presumably chosen to account for variations in body proportions, sizes and shapes. But had the squares been, say, 8cm x 8cm, then far more of them would have fitted in to the unwrapped area of the human body. That would have significantly increased the probability against the findings being chance, in this case to 1 in 40,000. So in my view the actual odds as stated have to be treated with caution, as they are a function of the size of the square that was chosen, not just the proximity of the wound sites. In a sense the odds in themselves do not matter; they are just an indicator to demonstrate the consistency of the birthmark/wound proximity. The importance of the paper lies in the overall investigation and the fact that it gives us solid empirical evidence that information of some sort is passed from one life to the next.

Dear David

Thank you very much for the paper by Dr Stevenson, which I found fascinating and which I read to my father who is ancient Brahmin but also quite deaf who also found it interesting and which makes me think that now the evidence of a continuation of consciousness after death is proven beyond reasonable doubt and to such a degree that now it would be an unreasonable person who denies it although I am sure many people of certain characteristics will continue to deny it because of the mind-set they have and the need to stay with simplistic and narrow paradigm that they are familiar with so there is nothing one can say to such people because you cannot use reason to argue against an unreasonable position.

I think one of most interesting aspects of Dr Stevenson's work is that he has placed time-bomb under conventional thinking and he has shown that the old spiritual paradigm that required faith is outmoded and now we do not need to 'believe' in the old way or trust our guru or priest or Iman as we can fall back on a reasoned argument that can be deduced from empirical data. This has obvious advantages as it over-rides old arguments about spiritual matters and it means that sensible people can have sensible ideas and create a world view and a value system based more on truth and less on emotional needs or dogma.

There is incidentally one area where perhaps evidence of reincarnation is observable to each of us, and that is field of linguistics because behavioural psychologists have for decades been intrigued by the way children acquire language; they learn their first language in a way and at a rate of progress that far outstrips any other learning process so by age of five most children have a fairly accurate grasp of complex rules of grammar and syntax and they pick it up easily, spontaneously and non-intellectually with little or no input from adults.

This has led some scientists and academics such as Noam Chomsky to postulate that there is some sort of 'universal language' or innate language learning ability within each of us that somehow helps us to acquire our language skills so they theorise that our brain is somehow configured in a way that allows these skills to be rapidly developed.

But what if this process is simply an influence that we each have brought with us from a previous life? Everyone uses language hundreds of times a day whether speaking or listening, reading or writing so it is reasonable to suppose, indeed certain, that we did exactly same in our previous lives and we have probably been using and honing our language skills for many lifetimes. We enter this world as linguistic veterans and our previous experience guides us, even if new language is different from earlier one so as soon as our physical body is capable we take to language effortlessly and skilfully because we have done it many times before.

Could reincarnation be an explanation? Certainly the inherent language talents of infants are not explained by current theories and there is strong evidence that we bring much more with us into this life than physical body because we know with some certainty that birthmarks are a carry-over from a previous life so if this can happen with something as clear and tangible as birthmark, why not language?

Thank you once again for bringing this paper to my attention.

Yours sincerely, K Ramana

Chapter 8

Connections

Dear Dr Ramana,

I have suddenly been able to see this whole idea of karma with a quite startling clarity. I have to say that I suspect you have been feeding me ideas and then patiently waiting for me to piece things together. Well, I am pleased to say I got there in the end! The connection hit me whilst cycling home from work. A light bulb lit up inside my head. A number of things now seem quite obvious.

It is now clear to me that each of us creates our own karma in this life, by way of our thought patterns. I see examples of it in friends and acquaintances whose circumstances obviously reflect the state of mind they have held for large parts of their lives. The connection between a mental attitude and the eventual outcome is quite plain to see.

We have established that reincarnation is a fact, a fact based upon reliable evidence. We also know that information such as birthmarks, language, memories and phobias somehow gets transferred to a new life and that a lot of this, especially the birthmarks, is tangible and measurable. We can thus have confidence in this knowledge.

So, it is very reasonable to argue that our thoughts, meaning our intentions, our loves and hates, our desires, can also get carried over into our next life. Why shouldn't they? Many other things do. And that is the law of karma. What we think in this life, our thoughts, intentions and desires, will determine what will happen to us in this life, and our next life. *And our circumstances in this life, our karma, have probably been, to some extent at least, determined by our thought patterns in an earlier life.*

It's all rational. The law of karma stands up to analysis and scrutiny. It is logical. It is not dependent on belief or dogma and does not require faith or reliance on a guru's insight. There is such a thing as karma. Your thoughts in this life eventually influence the way you will be reborn, the circumstances, the challenges you must face. We each create it for ourselves, with our thoughts.

This gives us a whole new way of looking at things. Any problems I may encounter in this life are of my own making; I created them, with my thoughts, at an earlier time. It is perfectly clear that my destiny and my future happiness are entirely my own responsibility. And morality, for example, now has a thoroughly sound basis; there is a tangible reason why we should all behave correctly towards each other. We have a precious opportunity to do good here and now, and it will benefit everyone, others presently and ourselves in the future. And if a person does harm to us we have no need to retaliate; that person's harmful intentions will come back to them at some point.

And we can be fairly sure that the evil and selfish people of the world will one day become aware of the pain they have caused. They will be obliged to re-evaluate their actions, as they inevitably discover the extent and impact they have had on others. Their own thoughts would make sure of it. This is borne out by the testimony of people who have undergone Near Death Experiences. Many of them described what could be called a panoramic life review, when the experiencer was shown his whole life in a vivid way. They clearly see the hurt they have caused others during their life, and they also witness the joy and happiness they created. This shows us that there is an intrinsic and natural moral order at work in the universe.

There is more! The law of karma neatly resolves the age old philosophical debate about free will and determinism. Karma suggests that free will is about our future; determinism is our here-and-now. By that I mean that we have the freedom to decide our future by the way we think today, but our current circumstances and characteristics have been determined by our mental attitude, the choices we made, at an earlier time. So there is no contradiction between free will and determinism; it is just a case of different influences applying at different times. As Buddha once said, 'What we are today comes from our thoughts of yesterday, and our present thoughts build our life of tomorrow. Our life is our creation of our mind.'

And, perhaps most importantly, these ideas have a sound, rational basis. I don't have to 'believe' in it; it is the logical outcome of empirical data. I do not need a guru or a scripture. I do not need to rely on the ideas, the dogma, of other people. I do not need to abide by a moral code that has been foisted upon me by medieval holy men. Karma does not require faith.

So I must thank you sincerely for guiding me in this direction, and also for allowing me to figure it out for myself. The best lessons are those that you learn for yourself. But I suspect that someone such as yourself has a much deeper and more esoteric way of looking at karma.

With best wishes, David

Chapter 9

A Wave on an Ocean

The letter I received from Dr Ramana a month later required some editing on my part. It was poorly written and quite confusing, and as the concepts he was trying to convey were somewhat abstract, I decided it would benefit from some tidying up. The essence of the letter, however, remains true to the original.

Dear David

I am glad you have figured it out for yourself because discovering things in this way is of huge value in contrast to those who simply follow blindly what they are told to believe by others.

Of course, there is much more cosmic way of understanding it as it is the force of nature that ultimately creates everything around us and that force originates in our thoughts; in our consciousness. This is an important aspect of our understanding, so I will try to explain it from a Hindu viewpoint.

Imagine a wave on an ocean and imagine for a moment that this wave can think, that it somehow has sense of self, and that it can look around at the world outside itself. It would look upon other waves as being separate from itself and it would perhaps compare its own size with the size of other waves, compare its own power with the power in others, indeed it might feel intimidated by bigger waves and feel arrogant when it found itself to be the biggest wave in the neighbourhood.

Now supposing this remarkable, imaginary wave began to grow in its awareness. As its consciousness expands it slowly and spontaneously begins to suspect that it is in fact part of something much bigger, so that instead of being separate from all the other waves it realises that maybe they are all connected and all come from the same source, so it looks around at other waves and feels connected to them. It eventually sees that it is not limited to this small self but is in fact nothing more and nothing less than the ocean itself. It recognises that the ocean is huge, of unfathomable depth and of enormous power. It sees that the power the individual wave has, and all the waves around it have, is because they are one, they are all part of a unified whole. That ocean is consciousness.

That is the relationship between self and Self, between the relative and the absolute, or between atman and Brahman, whichever terms you choose to use. In a sense there is no relationship because the word relationship requires two parties whereas in this instance there is only one, a unity. You can describe your cousin as relation, but you cannot describe your arm as a relation because you and your arm are one, so in this way self with a small S is a part of Self.

The limited image of individuality that the wave once had is Maya, meaning an illusion brought about by the wave's egotism, its ignorance of its true self. This does not mean illusion in the sense of a mirage or magic trick but an illusion brought about simply by the wave's limited awareness, so if you were to view the ocean from the wave's position all the surface activity you see, such as waves rising, tumbling and merging, the wind and the storms and the currents, all this is maya. It is illusory because it is not the whole picture; you cannot see the still depths of the ocean beneath all that activity. It is a form of ignorance which propagates the illusion of separateness and it is this illusion of separateness that allows ignorant people to believe that they can harm others without doing harm to themselves. It is this ignorance of our true self that allows us to be indifferent to the plight of the starving millions, so that we see them as 'different' or 'separate' and not relevant to our lives, and it is this ignorance that allows us to be indifferent to the suffering of our wartime enemies, because we see them as remote and separate.

The dynamic force that drives this oceanic environment, the

energy behind and within the storms and tides, the waves and wind, all these forces which are created by our consciousness, is Karma.

The growth in awareness leads us to the realisation that our wave is an integral part of a transcendent whole, and this realisation is called Moksha. *It means 'release' in Sanskrit and describes the liberation of a person from ignorance and thus from* Samsara, *the eternal cycle of birth and rebirth. The individual wave is referred to as* Jiva, *a word that includes more than just a personal body but refers also to the eternal aspect of that person; the part that continues life after life. As Jiva grows in consciousness it ultimately recognises that it is part of the ocean, so it becomes* Atman. *The words Jiva and Atman are closely related and easily confused. Atman is the higher aspects of the individual Jiva, it is the part that has recognised the unity of all things.*

And the whole, the ocean in its depths and at its surface, in the intelligence contained within all things, the totality of all you can see and all that is beyond seeing, that is Brahman. *As atman realises its true self it becomes the all, meaning that it is Brahman.*

To grow in consciousness, to recognise maya for what it is: a mistake, a limited view that propagates the illusion of separateness and allows us to tolerate the suffering and starvation of others, and thus to move beyond the world of karma, towards a unity with Brahman, towards peace and compassion, this is the goal of meditation and yoga. The word yoga means union, and union is what it helps us to achieve.

Karma is a vast and subtle law of nature which pervades and encompasses our everyday existence to an extent we simply cannot realise, and it is very good thing that you are understanding it and how it affects your life.

Yours sincerely, K Ramana

This is classic Hindu philosophy, both in its content and the way it is expressed. Dr Ramana uses analogies about oceans of unfathomable depths, he talks of the totality of existence and how humans are tossed about in storms. But this analogy, abstract though it may seem, is in fact a description of our day-to-day lives. We can, at one end of the spectrum of personal growth, be nothing more than an individual wave, with a thousand illusions of importance, grandeur and sophistication. At the other end is someone who is in harmony with the people and circumstances that surround him. This person will invariably be at peace with himself, and thus with others. Things will naturally and effortlessly work out for him. People, even strangers, will feel at ease in his company. Such a person will be compassionate and wish to serve others, because the illusion of separateness will have dissolved.

The spectrum is in fact one of mental health; at one end lies egotism and ignorance, which results in suffering, at the other end lies peace and happiness, a sense of belonging or unity, being in harmony with the laws of nature, in a word: enlightenment. We are each located somewhere along this spectrum. Our position is initially determined by our karma, but is ultimately a function of our state of consciousness.

But these concepts, such as oceans and waves, are in fact very difficult for us to imagine. We do not see how they apply to us as individuals, in our day-to-day lives. We cannot understand it on an intellectual level; it has to be recognised in a different way to ordinary knowledge. It reminds me of Dr Ramana's letter about Einstein and the Ninth Symphony, the true understanding of which requires us to put the intellect to one side temporarily. We can only 'experience' this sort of knowledge, and know it in a purely intuitive way. This is, of course, fraught with dangers. Many people claim, for example, to have had revelations, that 'God has spoken to me,' and use this to justify all sorts of bizarre beliefs, dogmas and behaviour. I suspect that we will only 'see' Dr Ramana's concepts clearly and truly when we have evolved to a greater degree of enlightenment, and our consciousness is not distorted by hidden contaminants.

While Hindus may be descriptive and speculative, Buddhists are, it seems, much more practical and down-to-earth. They would perhaps describe the difference like this: imagine you have been shot in the arm with an arrow; instead of speculating on who fired it and why, Buddhists would emphasise the importance of the wound being treated immediately. Who injured you does not have an immediate relevance when you are in pain. This practical approach recognises that life can be difficult for many people and a cure is necessary, without wasting effort on abstract discussion. There is nothing contradictory about these two positions; they are just different perspectives of the same concept, one broad and dramatic, the other specific and realistic.

Buddha, in the earlier quote, refers to an impure and a pure mind, and it is this quality of mind that determines the type of karma we create. Buddha doesn't use the words impure or pure in a moral or virtuous sense, he is not advocating piety as a means of obtaining a positive outcome. He is in fact talking about the *quality of consciousness*, a mind free of deep negative influences such as hatred, selfishness and fear. This is a huge subject, and an important one too, as it governs everything we experience.

The contaminants that corrupt our nervous system, our means of thinking, could collectively be referred to as stress. Everyone has stress in their nervous system to a greater or lesser extent. Many of us appear to bring that stress with us when we are born, and most of us accrue more stress in our childhood. And all of us collect stress in our day to day lives. We may for example be late for an appointment and get stuck in a traffic jam. Pressures of work or parenthood may overwhelm us and financial matters can be an enormous burden. Divorce and bereavement are hugely stressful. And for some of us there are exceptionally stressful periods in our lives; those caught up in the tragedy of war may never fully recover. These stresses have a huge impact on our lives and, importantly, the way we think. Our personality is to a large extent shaped by the various combinations of stresses we have experienced during our lives.

When our nervous system is overburdened with stress a number of things happen. We may become short tempered and impatient, indeed in extremes we may become full of anger and hatred. Our decision-making process is impaired and this can have huge consequences. Our discrimination skills reduce, so the perspective we take on moral or philosophical issues may be distorted. And we invariably find ourselves becoming egocentric; this is a natural response to perceived threats.

In Dr Ramana's analogy of the wave, we see that the distortions and egocentricity that the wave may develop as a result of these stresses will dictate the view it has of the world around it. Instead of having a wholesome sense of unity with the ocean that it is in fact a part of, and a kinship with the other waves, it will feel separate and alienated. It will experience what we could perhaps call a cosmic loneliness.

One of the first responses to stress, as basic as the fight-or-flight instinct, is to become selfish. We sometimes see individuals who have inner issues or stresses; they often lead a life devoid of warmth or affection, full of selfishness and self-indulgence. Also, if our wave were to feel threatened by the surrounding larger waves it might compensate with an exaggerated sense of its own importance.

With this state of mind we create our world. We create our karma. The process is totally independent of an ethical code; it is simply a law of nature, of cause and effect. The law of gravity is a good example for comparison. If I fall out of a twenty storey window I will hit the ground and be killed. There is no judgement involved in this. God is not in his heaven observing my accident and deciding that I have contravened a specific rule and therefore deserve a certain type of retribution. I hit the ground and I die; blame, justice and punishment are not part of the unfolding of this event. There is no such thing as 'bad' gravity. It is simply gravity, a law of nature.

Similarly if I spend a lifetime being selfish, angry or confrontational, those thoughts will somehow create the circumstances for me to eventually reap the result, either in this life or the next. I am not being punished by a third party nor by a remote immutable law; I am simply attracting a specific result. If I give out love and kindness the same mechanism will come into play and love and kindness is what nature will give back to me.

Another way to describe it is that I am being punished *by* my mistakes, not *for* my mistakes. This is a subtle but important distinction. Having fallen from a high window, I am not being punished *for* my carelessness, I am being punished *by* my carelessness. There is no moral code involved, no set of rules, no third party. In fact I am not being *punished* at all, as the word implies a value judgement. I am simply receiving the effect of my actions.

This is the philosophy of karma. It differs fundamentally from the Christian, Muslim or Judaic viewpoint, where a person is apparently judged by a God or according to a set of commandments, and is then punished or rewarded accordingly. With karma things simply happen in accordance with the laws of nature. It is our own responsibility. We each create our own heaven and hell.

Chapter 10

Meditation

By now it had become clear to me that meditation is an intrinsic part of Eastern philosophy. I studied a number of books on the subject and spoke to various people who claimed to have an understanding of it. There are of course numerous types of meditation and one has to find a type that feels comfortable. The advice I was given was to learn a meditation technique that was effortless and easy in its practice; to force or coerce the mind was regarded as unnatural and therefore counter-productive.

The consensus was that you cannot learn meditation from a book; it has to be taught formally, on a one-to-one basis. I enrolled on a short course and began to practise it regularly. Not much seemed to happen and I felt deflated. I would sometimes meditate and find myself thinking about other things for the whole twenty minutes. I would tell my tutor that nothing was happening; he would laugh and assure me that it was. He was a likeable chap who began every sentence with the word 'So.'

It is hard to quantify and describe the benefits. Changes took place gradually and at a subtle level. As the months passed I seemed to soften, to be more tolerant. Many everyday things began to gradually lose their importance: I ceased to worry about money, or the future. I stopped regretting silly things from the past and lived very much in the here-and-now. As my consciousness became more stress free so my way of looking at the world evolved. I began to find any form of cruelty abhorrent and unnecessary, any kind of selfishness distasteful. I felt slightly detached from everything, yet paradoxically I felt I understood more. I no longer worried about other peoples' opinions of me. I wasn't indifferent or aloof; I just wasn't concerned.

I suppose the most significant change was that I now valued

silence above all else. During meditation I would sometimes experience a deep inner quietness, a delicious sense of relief, a transcendent feeling of self containment, as though I was beyond suffering, fear or desire. I gradually understood the motivation of the Buddhist monk or Hindu recluse, and their need to quietly walk away from the noisy fripperies of everyday life and turn their attention within. I began to love the still beauty of eternal silence. Sometimes I would reach a quietness of such exquisite purity that even Mozart seemed vulgar.

I wrote to Dr Ramana and told him that I had learned to meditate.

I am very pleased to hear this (he replied) *as you would be limiting your personal growth without it, but you must realise that meditation found you, you did not find meditation, because the time was right for you to learn, so nature provided you with that opportunity.*

For many years I taught people to meditate. I learnt as child as it is part of our family tradition, and have always practised it regularly and studied it because it is fascinating area of knowledge, especially for somebody like me in the medical profession, so I often taught patients from the hospital, especially when I could see that their medical problems had an emotional component.

Meditation is an aspect of yoga, and in fact the word yoga means union; it is means of attaining unity with the cosmos and it is not specifically an Indian idea any more than gravity is English because of your Mr Newton's place of birth and neither is it denominational which means it is not exclusively Hindu nor Buddhist nor anything else, and its practice and understanding is open to anyone. Yoga is not belief system but a technique and it depends solely upon the laws of nature and is means for attaining an improved state of consciousness, one that ultimately allows us to experience a holistic and all-embracing sense of union with all of creation. It burns up the seeds of karma, so that eventually you attain the highest form of freedom.

Yoga is a branch of Ayurveda, which means knowledge of life but there are numerous other Vedas and they are the oldest scriptures ever compiled and form the basis of Hinduism but remember the word Veda simply means knowledge but the essence of yoga is the practice of it, the experience. I am told that your western usage of the word seems to be confined to people doing stretching exercises in the village hall but it is in fact much broader and more profound body of knowledge than that and provides complete and holistic discipline for physical, mental and spiritual wellbeing with meditation being a significant part.

Some folk, for example Himalayan sadhus and lamas, take this process to higher level by devoting their entire lives to meditation and in some cases achieving higher state of consciousness as their nervous system becomes ever more free of stress and its damaging effects and they live life of bliss, which takes them beyond fear.

During the long periods of deep meditation when virtually all activity in their brain has ceased these yogis subjectively experience a profound, all-enveloping silence and at this level of consciousness they are able to recognise a value system that is in total harmony with the laws of nature and they can do this because they are listening to their own mind at a much finer, more natural level, so they are receptive to the delicate thoughts that would in anybody else be drowned away by the radio-like buzz and interference of a damaged nervous system, so the yogis are able to cognise the pure laws of nature because they are in unity with those laws, they are part of them, they can hear them, so when they do think something it is true and evolutionary as it has not suffered the distortions and blockages of a damaged mind during its journey towards outward expression.

Encouraged by the letter I began to read more about meditation. As Dr Ramana said, it is a fascinating body of knowledge. And I soon realised that it is in fact a vitally important factor in my efforts to understand karma.

The person regarded as the father of meditation is Sri Patanjali. He lived in India in the second century BCE and codified his knowledge in the form of sutras (the written word was not prevalent at that time). Sutras, or threads, are short, terse sentences that his students would learn by heart. Later, as they passed this knowledge on, they would elaborate and expand the sutra. In this way Patanjali's expertise has been handed down through the centuries in a fairly consistent way.

So what is meditation? It is essentially a way of turning the attention inwards, away from day to day distractions, and allowing the mind to withdraw and reach a very settled state. It is usually done with the help of a mantra, which is a subtle or sacred sound that may be chanted or repeated silently. It helps the mind to effortlessly settle down and step outside of its normal conceptual thinking. I had in fact previously heard of a couple of mantras: Om (or Aum, as it is sometimes spelled) and the Tibetan Om Mani Padme Hum, but I had been advised not to use them. Mantras are surprisingly powerful and using an incorrect one can do more harm than good.

Some schools use a visual symbol, known as a yantra. Zen practitioners contemplate a koan, a seemingly illogical statement that trips up the mind and causes it to think outside of everyday concepts. Whichever technique is employed it needs to be taught by a suitable teacher, and cannot generally be learned from a book.

Meditation works in a simple and natural way. The settled state a meditator experiences is a form of deep rest of a very subtle kind. This rest allows the stresses that are stored in the nervous system to be gradually and gently dissolved, which causes the whole physiology to heal and thus function more effectively. The benefits of meditation could take up a book in themselves, as could the explanations of how it works, and indeed many books have been written on the subject.

The results of this healing process can be seen at various levels; physical health, psychological wellbeing and spiritual unfoldment. These sound like three separate areas, but in fact they form a continuum of personal growth. The measurable health benefits include reduced blood pressure, improved resistance to illness and better sleep patterns. Psychological improvements include reduced anxiety, enhanced personal relationships and better concentration, to name but a few. But it is the spiritual benefits that are our principal concern here. These are difficult to quantify, but are tangible nonetheless.

When a person has been meditating for some time they may begin to notice subtle and spontaneous changes in their relationship with the world. They find over the months and years that conflict, both personal and in a broader sense, is viewed as a futile and unnecessary activity; they value peace and tolerance much more. They prefer to avoid aggressive people and noisy places. They often reduce their alcohol and meat consumption, not out of any high moral standing but simply because it feels right. They will usually report that they are happier and more content within themselves, and that this happiness is not dependent on status or material possessions. They may describe themselves as being spiritual, as distinct from religious. Each of these changes occurs spontaneously and gradually; they are not necessarily the result of conscious decisions. And they are independent of IQ or educational attainment.

What brings about this beneficial change in a person's thinking? The way we think is to a large extent decided by the health of our nervous system. As we contact the deeper, more silent parts of the mind during meditation our stresses are slowly but surely soothed out of existence by the deep rest, so our thinking, and thus the way we interface with the world, becomes easier and more harmonious. It is not corrupted or distorted by stress. This is a totally natural process and does not require effort, belief or intellectual input. Permanent neuronal changes are known to take place in long term meditators within the left pre-frontal cortex of the brain and the amygdala. This effect has been clinically proven and it leads to a reduction in cognitive dissonance, or the disharmony in a person's life that ultimately expresses itself as unhappiness.

Meditators, it seems, fall into two broad categories: householders and recluses. A householder may have a job and a family, and meditation takes up only a small amount of his time. A recluse, for example a Hindu or Buddhist monk, is a person who has decided to devote his or her life to spiritual endeavour. He may therefore spend many hours each day in meditation, and will not have the domestic distractions that a householder has.

It is difficult to know exactly what experiences a recluse enjoys, for various reasons. Firstly, any experience is deeply subjective and thus difficult to describe. Secondly, a meditator soon learns not to discuss these matters as he may receive a sneering response from people who do not understand it. Thirdly, when a person has achieved considerable spiritual evolution his ego will have diminished to such an extent that he will not wish to talk about himself or his experiences. Sri Aurobindo, for example, when asked if he was enlightened, replied that it was an impossible question to answer. He said that the word 'enlightened' and the word 'I' cannot coexist in the same sentence, because for an enlightened person there is no such thing as I. There are no individual waves, just the ocean.

But some spiritually evolved teachers, such as Sri Aurobindo, Maharishi Mahesh Yogi and Ramana Maharshi, will in fact describe these experiences in an attempt to guide others. They may talk about a profound sense of peace and compassion, and will relate feelings of unity with the whole cosmos, as though they have become a part of it and are inseparable from it. They look at a flower and intuitively feel no sense of separateness between them, and they see within the flower a clear expression of nature's intelligence. They have an intuitive understanding that everything in the universe is somehow unified and cannot be separated into discrete components. They see that love is the power that unifies and guides all of creation.

So what is happening here? Why are these changes taking place? This is a huge and difficult question. The meditator may describe how, during meditation, his mind sinks to a deeper and deeper level of silence until eventually there is no activity in his mind, just the white screen of pure consciousness. This state is known as Samadhi and, it is claimed, is the source of all thought. It is a boundless silence. It is the place where everything we think originates and is regarded by yogis and mystics as being the home of all the laws of nature. The meditator is at this point completely in harmony, in unity, with nature's laws.

Regular and prolonged contact with this boundless state will result in a sense of unity being suffused into the day to day life of the meditator. He will eventually perceive the universe, indeed all of creation, as a seamless, interconnected whole, even when he is not meditating. He will not experience fear, because fear belongs at the grosser levels of the mind, where consciousness has been contaminated by negativity. Because he is so identified with the home of all nature's laws, any thoughts, feelings and intuition that he experiences during periods of meditation will be positive and life supporting, for the simple reason that they have not been corrupted by the stresses experienced at the grosser levels of the mind. Each thought will be a pure expression of nature; that's all it can be.

Chapter 11

Akasha - The Universe's Memory

By now I had a rudimentary understanding of what karma is. The puzzle that I was now faced with was: how does it work? For example, how is information transferred from one life to the next? What mechanisms are in place, presumably embedded in the laws of nature, to determine the circumstances of a new life? How do thoughts actually affect the physical world around us?

These seemed to me to be huge questions. I wrote to Dr Ramana and asked for the Vedic perspective. That would be a good place to start and then perhaps I could try to understand it from a Western point of view.

He replied:

The term used to describe this process of transferring information from one life to next is samskara, *and these are often referred to as the seeds of karma, or we can liken them to a briefcase that we bring with us when we arrive in this new life that contains all the knowledge, information and intelligence from previous lives. Samskaras can be described as the deep impressions or character-istics which will influence what we eventually become.*

Where does the knowledge reside prior to the briefcase? Well, the briefcase is in a sense the focussed, condensed information that always resides within Akasha, *which is the Sanskrit term for space, although it in fact means much more than your Western usage of the word and is more like your Victorian word* ether, *which was a medium postulated to explain how light and radio waves travelled through vacuum; akasha is similar, but it is omniscient not empty and it is all-pervading and imperceptible. Akasha is in a sense the universe's memory and the Vedas claim that every thought that every person has ever had is recorded in akasha, every thought, deed and desire of every person in every life, and these records influence the circumstances of our next incarnation, being deeply embedded tendencies or influences waiting to become active, that determine the reality that we will experience, so remember, the word karma means 'action' and the samskaras are effectively the seeds for that action that you bring with you from your past.*

(Storing information in this way is not in fact such a fanciful idea. In the subatomic world information is stored at a sublimely microscopic level. Particles somehow know how to behave; that knowledge, that intelligence, must be retained somewhere. In quantum theory the very finest level of creation is nothing more than a field of pure intelligence; it is the home of all the laws of nature and everything in the world emanates from it. This is where particles obtained their characteristics, and thus know where to be at a specific time. Hence the idea of akasha is not so very far removed from the theories of modern-day physics).

Dr Ramana continued...

Of course, there are many other factors that influence us such as genetics, the environment and world history but how we respond to our environment for example or the historical time we live in depends upon our samskaras, that collection of talents, fears, desires etc. that we have brought with us.

These samskaras are the seeds of our new life and as the infant grows so the seeds flower into the circumstances, characteristics and events of that life and the direction it takes, but these seeds can be overridden; they can effectively be burnt up, so that we can be free of the influences that are burdening us and trapping us in this endless cycle of birth and re-birth.

If you remember in my ocean analogy, I described karma as the dynamic force that drives all the activity and events that happen to us in our lives and I said that by practising meditation we expand our awareness to such an extent that our individual ego diminishes and eventually disappears. As this happens we are effectively burning the seeds of karma, we slowly become aware that we are much more than an individual ego (wave) and are part of something much more vast and powerful (the ocean) and so the samskaras therefore become less potent and eventually lose their influence and we are then beyond karma, and that is the path to enlightenment.

I have in this way given you eastern description of this process but as we have discussed many times there is always other viewpoint, which is the western scientific view, and I would be very grateful if you could tell me how you in the west would see this issue as I am always very interested to understand things from different perspective.

Yours sincerely, K Ramana

Dear Dr Ramana,
The idea of akasha and samskaras was new to me and was, I must admit, difficult to accept. How is this information stored, or transmitted to wherever it is needed? Were the birthmarks found on the children in Dr Stevenson's study placed there by means of samskaras?

I suspect the answer resides in the very structure of our brain. The Western view is, of course, somewhat different to yours, but I am beginning to understand how quantum physics has a degree of commonality with the Eastern viewpoint. I have read a number of books on this subject and am starting to see the similarities between east and west. My viewpoint is, I have to admit, rudimentary and simplistic, but I will explain the best I can.

Years ago, many people thought the brain was simply a hugely complex and powerful computer. This view is largely discredited now. Sir Roger Penrose, a distinguished and respected Oxford physicist, claims that the known laws of physics are unable to explain the phenomenon of consciousness. Physics can explain how a computer works, but the brain is entirely different. A thought *experiment quickly shows that this is in fact quite obvious; if we were to place in a test tube all the components of a brain, the cells, the myriad of chemicals such as neuro-transmitters, the minute electrical charges, the blood supply and so on, would the test tube begin to think? I doubt it very much. Consciousness is not explainable in terms of the physical properties of the brain. How consciousness works is simply not understood − indeed it is not even clear which area of knowledge it falls into. Is it neuro-science? Philosophy? Advanced computer science? Quantum physics?*

Pictures of a human brain show a doughy-looking object, shaped a bit like a grey and spongy cauliflower, and this is of course correct at that level of observation. But delve deeper into it, with ever more powerful microscopes, and it looks very different. It eventually becomes a swirling mass of cells and chemicals, with minute electrical signals firing off in all directions. This is, of course, something you will be far more familiar with than I am, but please bear with me as this helps me to understand some new and complex ideas.

The brain, like everything else in the human body, is made up of cells. The cells consist of molecules, which are in turn made of atoms. These atoms are unimaginably small; if the point of a pin was expanded to the size of a dome over a football stadium, an atom resting on that pinpoint would be about the size of an apple pip. Although atoms are usually referred to as particles, they are not particles in the sense that a grain of sand is a particle They are in fact minute electrical charges, and they often behave in a way that is bizarre and illogical. The atom has a nucleus, which is surrounded by a swarm of electrons, the number of which deter-mines the atom's characteristics. The nucleus consists of a proton and a neutron, which are made of yet smaller components, such as quarks. Ultimately, it is thought, they consist of loops of vibrating strings, though that again is a convenient image rather than a concrete description. They have no material form in the normal sense; they are best described as pure intelligence.

To me the most intriguing aspect of this is the fact that these strings and particles somehow know *how to combine with other strings and particles to form matter as we see it in our everyday world. They don't just swirl around at random. They contain within themselves the intelligence to join together in very specific way, trillions and trillions of them. From a field of nothingness they dance together like a huge swarm of bees, combining and forming complex and intricate patterns until collectively they form matter. Whether we look at a colourful orchid or a song thrush, or the perfect features of a newborn child, everything we see has emanated in a miraculous way from a field of intelligence that is the foundation of all of life.*

At this miniscule level of creation the conventional laws of physics appear to break down. The world no longer behaves as we are used to in our everyday life. This is the quantum world and conventional thinking, Newton's Laws of Motion for example, simply do not apply. These sub-atomic particles cannot be said to exist in a specific place; we can only approximate their location and quantify it in terms of the probability of it being there. And these particles have a strange, fuzzy existence. They are not like the tree in my back garden, which is in a particular place and remains there all day whilst I am at work, and is still there when I get home in the evening. A particle in the quantum world only seems to reveal itself, only become manifest, when an observer focuses on it; consciousness is a fundamental part of this process. At other times it assumes a strange twilight existence. It is there, somewhere, but we can only approximate its location; it needs consciousness to make it 'real.'

Sir James Jeans (1877-1946), a physicist, astronomer and Professor of Applied Mathematics at Princeton University said in an interview published in The Observer (London):

I incline to the idealistic theory that consciousness is fundamental, and that the material universe is derivative from consciousness, not consciousness from the material universe. It may well be, it seems to me, that each individual consciousness ought to be compared to a brain-cell in a universal mind.

These bizarre particles are what our brains are made of; this is the structure of the organ we each think with. At a level that is so small that even the most powerful microscope won't help us, the brain is a fizzing mass of contradictions, a dreamlike world where particles flicker in and out of existence, and where the idea of space and time has no meaning. At this, the very smallest, subtlest level of matter, the particles that make up our brain do not conform to the everyday laws of space-time that we normally accept as an intrinsic part of our day-to-day existence. The commonsense framework within which we structure our perception of the world simply does not exist here. There is no such thing as space.

So we are doing our thinking with an organ that is, in a sense, everywhere and nowhere at the same time. It is part of an interconnected web of information. It has no spatial definition. This is very difficult for us to imagine, as our whole perceptual framework is built upon the idea of things existing at a specific point in three dimensional space; that is how we have viewed the world since the day we were born. In the quantum world, matter is in fact like the analogy of the ocean; the waves all appear separate and distinct, but when we see the whole picture each wave is just a local manifestation of the huge, fathomless sea. All waves are in a sense united, a part of the same whole. They appear as individual outbreaks of energy and activity when seen in isolation, but the complete picture is somewhat different. There is only unity.

The Vedas talk in terms of unity, the physicist talks of an absence of space. It is the same thing. Countless quantum physicists have described the material world in almost identical terms as the ancient rishis. They claim that the universal interconnectedness of objects and events is fundamental to atomic reality. David Bohm, one of the leading figures in this field, writes, '...we say that inseparable quantum interconnectedness of the whole universe is the fundamental reality, and that relatively independently behaving parts are merely particular and contingent forms within this whole.' Though written by a twentieth century physicist, this description could have come directly from the Vedas. Erwin Schrodinger, one of the world's greatest physicists, Nobel Prize winner (1933) and the father of quantum theory said, 'Quantum physics thus reveals a basic one-ness of the universe.'

So what conclusions can we draw from this long and convoluted letter? It is simply this: the description of reality from two entirely separate perspectives, the spiritual and the scientific, are remarkably similar. The Western scientific view validates the Eastern spiritual view. This allows us to have confidence in the truth of the Vedic model of reality and we do not need to resort to faith or dogma.

With best wishes, David

Dear David.

Thank you for your letter, which I found useful and thought provoking. So we must ask, what exactly is this interconnected web of information that our mind is a part of? In Vedic terms it is akasha so in my analogy I used the ocean as a means of describing Brahman, the totality of all things and akasha, as I understand it, is a specific aspect of that totality; it is effectively the recorded history, the information of all that has ever happened, including our thoughts. Our brain does not have access to that information in the normal sense; that would imply that the brain is in one place, the information in another, and the brain somehow accesses it whereas in fact the brain is the information and the information is the brain; they are both part of the same whole, they are all pieces of one omniscient web of interconnectedness and so there is no separation.

So why aren't we all aware of the information that's available in this non-localised source? Well we probably are, but the inadequacies of our nervous system are preventing us from realising it because our nervous system, meaning our brain and everything connected to it, is riddled with stress such as anger, anxiety, fear, regrets, fatigue, rejection, disappointment, all these factors accumulate within us and act as a barrier to the awareness of this subtle intelligence. It is like the background noise that interferes with a radio programme; if it gets too loud we lose the clarity and eventually we cannot understand anything.

Akasha then is an intrinsic, inescapable part of who we are; it is not a separate 'library' of facts and history, and samskaras are the local condensations of that universal information as it applies specifically to the individual and Dr Stevenson's birthmark research gives us tangible evidence that this is the case.

So what is the mechanism that allows these samskaras to transfer from one life to another? How does this intelligence manifest in a new body at different times? This is a complex subject.

Firstly, the concept of time is not entirely as we imagine it, which is a difficult notion to get our heads around because time is, to many physicists, a construct of the human mind, one that allows us to see things in sequence, so that A is followed by B, which is followed by C and so on and in this way we can comprehend the world around us; for example the idea of cause and effect makes sense. But time may not be as simple as that because in some areas of quantum knowledge it takes on a different quality and indeed it ceases to exist in the normal sense of the word.

Akasha, where the information is stored, is a transcendental concept in that it is outside of the relative form of existence and is thus beyond time so to talk about a new body, or a sequence of bodies is perhaps to misinterpret the concept of time.

But nonetheless we do find ourselves in a new body so perhaps we should see this process as similar to a row of candles, one of which is burning and we use that candle to light the next one, and use that one to light the next and so on. They are all different and separate candles but in a sense it is the same flame; it has simply been passed on. As each flame burns it does so in accordance with the laws of nature and eventually each candle can no longer support the flame and it dies. The point here is that the part that gets passed on from candle to candle is the intelligence (in this case the intelligence of combustion) but with the human body the intelligence that gets passed on is the information called samskaras.

I hope this will give you some food of thought. These are simply my ideas based on a limited knowledge but the similarities between the western quantum theory and eastern philosophy would fill a book on their own, but I hope what I have written here will provide a small insight.

Yours sincerely, K Ramana

Intelligence, information, clearly does get passed on from one life to the next. Dr Stevenson's research on birthmarks confirms this to a reasonable degree. But I have to say I did not find Dr Ramana's letter very helpful. I was trying to understand the process of samskara and, whilst I can see the analogy of a flame being passed from candle to candle, it is only an illustration and does not in itself explain how it actually happens.

The birthmarks fascinated me. Here, for the first time in history, was tangible, reliable evidence that this life is not our first and that information can be carried over from one life to the next. It obviously happens, but how?

Chapter 12

Karma and Dharma

Dear Dr Ramana

It now seems clear to me as an outsider that samskaras do have some influence on our personal characteristics, though to what degree I'm not sure. Clearly this will have an effect on our subsequent circumstances; for example if I bring a huge musical talent with me into this world, this may dictate my career path. But does that apply to everyone? Is everybody's life mapped out by the events or desires we had in a previous life? Do we not have free will?

He replied:

We start from premise that we are here on this earth as part of our growth and our evolution because according to Dr Moody we are here to learn, and more importantly, to learn to love, to give love and to receive love which is not an easy thing for many of us to do, and it often takes many lifetimes to achieve it. We can see that each of us is at different stage so some are very loving and compassionate, many are fairly neutral and some sad souls are full of selfishness and anger, so we all have task ahead of us. We also know that we evolve as families, even if my learned father tell me that this is not part of Vedic teaching and is dismissive and says it is far too New Age for his taste, but nonetheless we are each here to help our family and friends to evolve and we help them with their lessons and they help us, because our circumstances are such that we come into contact with the appropriate people for this ongoing process of mutual growth, so we have in fact chosen our parents, and for very good reason although we usually do not realise this at the time. And the life around us, our financial, political and environmental circumstances, are also there to help us although we may not like them very much but they are what we need at that particular point in our development so for example if you were once selfish and unscrupulous with money maybe you now have to experience what it is like to be deprived.

We must always remember that karma is natural learning process, it is law of nature, not a trial or a punishment; there is no right or wrong, good or bad; everything is in its proper place to help us learn and evolve, and to help others do the same. Some people are born with difficult karmic path ahead of them, and it is quite normal for someone who loves them to accompany them on this journey even at expense of their own happiness and that person will always benefit because to help others with their struggle is always huge karmic advantage.

Let us take a typical family, and see how this karmic mutual assistance works. A child is born into dysfunctional family and let's say that the father has personality difficulties; he is always angry and has difficulty in showing his family love and affection and there is continual disharmony in the family home and as result the child grows up with emotional issues, falls behind at school, has difficult relationships and maybe needs psychological help to learn to deal with them. The mother, who is basically kind and loving, has to cope with continual anger being directed towards her and suffers from guilt about the effects this disharmony has on her child so she has often thought about leaving the father but has loyally stuck by him.

Now let us speculate on the real story, the bigger karmic picture, behind all of this, so let us say the father had accumulated karmic debts in previous lifetimes because he had been selfish and perhaps unkind, even cruel so he has lessons to learn and so nature gives him another opportunity, another life, to learn the things he previously misunderstood or missed. He is faced with life ahead of him that will not have much in the way of comfort or happiness; the lessons may be hard so his karmic influence will lead him to be born into difficult circumstances, such as incompetent parents or a war-torn environment.

But help is at hand and someone close to him want to help and so they decide to accompany him into this life, and as the father faces his karmic challenges the mother is there to offer solace and perhaps guidance. They meet not by accident as they had supposed but by design and she shows him love, which is what he is here to learn about so this is her life's purpose, her dharma.

The child, let's say it is a daughter, also has lessons to learn so she too has chosen her circumstances, chosen these parents and as she copes with the results of a disrupted childhood she evolves and gradually develops her own values, looking around and learning to recognise what is good and what is bad. Life is not always easy but she develops compassion especially for deprived children as she knows what they are going through, what they feel, and so as she grows she tries never to be selfish or unkind and later she tries to support her father in the declining years, and attempts to learn the lessons of forgiveness and letting go of the past and so she recognises that if life had been easy for her she would not have learned these important lessons.

The father eventually leaves this life perhaps with some discomfort given the karmic patterns he had created around himself and people at the funeral may comment on the difficulties he faced and quietly think to themselves that it must have been hard life, then later the wife follows her husband and decades later the daughter does so too.

Seen karmically, it was a win-win situation and though it may have looked challenging it was in fact hugely beneficial to all three family members. The father worked through his karmic debts, learned to value the love and support his family gave him, and understood perhaps how to give love in a small way, and consider for a moment what his life may have been like had he not had the support of a family, he could so easily have been overwhelmed, possibly turning to drink or crime, thus creating even more suffering and karmic debt. The wife supported her husband out of pure love so will have benefited enormously and the daughter has learned important lessons in her own life, has learned to value love, even if she cannot easily show it. She has understood many things, far more than the members of apparently functional and stable families around her.

So each of these family members has, in their own way, evolved, having helped each other, grown with each other and learned from each other's karmic path.

An interesting aside to all of this is the question of karma versus dharma. Dharma can be defined as actions in accord with the laws of nature, actions that enable a person to evolve effortlessly and in our example above we could say that the father's life was ruled by the laws of karma, the baggage that he brought with him into this life from earlier time. The mother, although compelled to be there by karmic forces, did what was beneficial to her husband and thus helped her own personal evolution so we could say she played a dharmic role as well.

The daughter is in fact more interesting as she is here to learn some hard lessons, but later in her life she learns these lessons gladly, with some degree of understanding and acceptance, so she has turned her karma to her advantage. She is therefore in a role that is both karmic and dharmic.

In fact it would be true to say that nobody's life is exclusively in one category or the other, rather we would say that there is a bias, with both influences applying to differing degrees. Karma was the driving force and was deterministic but in their between-lives state they all made choices (with free will) that fixed the circumstances of the lives they were about to experience, to ensure most learning.

I hope this illustration will give you something of a picture of how and why our lives unfold in the way that they do.

Yours sincerely, K Ramana

I could understand most of this, but the word dharma had me baffled, at least in Dr Ramana's use of the word. I looked it up and it seemed to mean the philosophy that was expounded by

Buddha, i.e. the core of Buddhist teachings. Yet Dr Ramana referred to people finding their dharma. Did that mean they had to find their own truth, their own fundamental philosophy? I wrote to him asking for clarification, and got a swift reply

The word dharma simply means Natural Law and the Buddhists do, as you say, use the word dharma in slightly different way to Vedic tradition; they mean the body of knowledge that leads to spiritual growth, or the essential, central teaching of Buddhism but in Vedanta dharma means something additional; it is concept you do not seem to have in West so there is not direct translation although some people think it is same as your English word 'duty' but dharma is in fact much more than duty it is duty performed happily and naturally and is the path that helps us in our spiritual evolution whereas duty in English usually means doing something that you do not like or indeed actively dislike but doing it anyway because there is moral or social obligation so a man may leave his family and go off to fight battles in muddy trenches for example, because he believes he is doing his duty, so he puts up with extreme suffering.

Dharma is similar but without the suffering and it means doing what is necessary in life to further one's evolution but doing it naturally, effortlessly and happily knowing that it is your role or your destiny to perform these actions so one talks of finding one's dharma, which is the right, natural thing for that person to do at that stage in his or her evolution, so it may be one person's dharma to be farmer, another's a soldier and another's a musician; it is what is right for them at that time.

Once when I was a child my father try to explain about dharma, so he took me into the garden and showed me bird building its nest and said, 'That is dharma, because the bird is free, happy and natural and it is building nest and having young because it wants to, not out of some imagined sense of duty so the bird's dharma is to propagate its own species and that's what it does, each year. It is happy performing its dharmic role – it isn't being intellectual, it hasn't thought about what it is doing and it hasn't had big debate on the whys and wherefores of child rearing, it simply does it and as it performs its actions it is united with nature; it is in harmony with the laws of nature.'

This is something the ancient seers of India understood when they wrote about it in Bhagavad Gita (Chapter 2, verse 48) that says 'Yogastha Kuru Karmani.' which means 'Established in yoga, perform action.' The word 'yoga' means union so it means being at one with nature, being in harmony with the laws of nature, with everything around you and this is the purpose of yoga and meditation, to gently bring you into harmony with the laws of nature and once you achieve that you will naturally find your dharma and so you will instinctively act in accordance with laws of nature instead of fighting against them which will ensure you achieve fulfilment and your behaviour will spontaneously be correct as you will be acting out your dharma.

Now I can hear you asking a big question: how do you know what is correct behaviour if you do not have moral code to refer to? Well, moral code is man-made concept, it is just an intellectual device to keep people comfortable and allow society to function reasonably well. The great seers did not need moral code because they were simply and spontaneously good and their compassion and goodness were natural part of them, just like their teeth or their hair and they had no need of list of rules created by others to tell them what to do or how to behave so their goodness is not something they strived for because it is natural, from deep within and I can assure you, going back to one of my earlier letters, they have not studied moral philosophy to discover what is good. That would make them laugh!

So I can hear you ask, how did they achieve that level of saintliness? Well firstly they would not regard it as saintliness; there is something smug about the word and it creates image of aloofness or superiority. No, the seers are good and compassionate because they have through years of yogic practices rid themselves of all the egotism, the anger, the fear, the envy, indeed anything that is negative or selfish, anything that causes unhappiness so they do not consider themselves superior; they see themselves as normal and healthy, with healthy nervous system. And the rest of us? We are to greater or lesser extent unhealthy, groping in the dark, full of fear and apprehension, hoping to find happiness in material possessions and ego gratification.

It is similar thing with humility and piety, which also cannot be learned from a book and cannot be rehearsed or practiced because it has to be genuine and it has to come from deep within so to just act with humility, to create an image of yourself as humble or pious is just acting and is another aspect of egotism, developed to make you feel superior to others. No, spiritually evolved person has natural humility which comes from within because years of yogic practice have slowly but surely dismantled the ego or what we in the east call the self so it is a question of quality of consciousness, not acting.

Ego is western word which I suppose it started with your Mr Freud. In India we often use the word self with a small S, as distinct from Self with large S, which can be little bit of confusing, but self with large S is the totality, the sum total of all reality, all of the cosmos, each and every god, all of intelligence and truth, it is the absolute, the underlying reality, the transcendental truth behind, inside and throughout everything but self with small S is the smaller you, an individual with an ego, with a thousand illusions and strong sense of me-ness, but it is also the source of discontent, of carrying the past with us in the form of regrets or guilt, and preoccupation with future such as anxiety about money. As the ego or self diminishes with continued meditation so these negative thought patterns naturally dissolve and we thus spontaneously begin to live in the here-and-now as we once did when we were child before we developed an ego, so that absence of ego explains why children have natural and innocent demeanour.

(Closing paragraph omitted).

If I understand this correctly, we could say that if a person is evolving, they are on their dharmic path, but if life is a struggle for them they are working through their karmic debts, their self inflicted difficulties.

For each of us, nature apparently presents a variety of circumstances and influences, and these may be karmic or dharmic by nature. Karmic influences have been predetermined by our earlier tendencies. Dharma is a matter of free will; we can each choose how we think and therefore how we behave. And these laws of nature override our surface-level desires; we do not usually see that this is something we must go through and learn from. Each of us would like a comfortable life, free from struggle and misfortune. But people with an easy life do not evolve significantly; they often become selfish and materialistic. It may seem like a good life superficially, but it is devoid of growth.

The solution appears to be simple, according to Dr Ramana. Regular meditation will naturally and easily take us in another direction, a direction where the small self outgrows its limitations and becomes a part of a bigger picture, the Self, where the wave becomes the ocean and where happiness and compassion are the norm. Meditation helps us find our dharma.

Chapter 13

Karma and Intention

Dear Dr Ramana
I have been re-reading your letter about dharma. Whilst I can
understand a lot of it, indeed most of it, I am puzzled by one thing:
I was surprised at your mention of a soldier in the context of
dharma. It seems incongruous. Is this not contrary to the ideal of
'ahimsa' (non-violence) as espoused by Mahatma Gandhi and The
Dalai Lama? Could a person who meditates be a soldier and even
take the life of another in battle? How can a person whose
occupation is based around the notion of killing others be said to
have found their dharmic path?
Regards, David

Dear David
There is in fact no contradiction in saying that soldier has found his
dharma, for being soldier is simply the right thing for the devel-
opment of that soul at that particular time so even though we may
think it is not very spiritual, in fact each of us is different and each
of us sees things from their own position, so no person can judge
another's dharma and so that particular person, that soldier, that
soul, has to undergo that experience as part of his evolution. His
profession is protecting others from attack by people with ill inten-
tions and if he is on his dharmic path then it is right for him to do
that, assuming he behaves correctly and is not wantonly cruel.
Don't forget, Arjuna, the hero of the Bhagavad Gita, was a soldier.
This may sound counter-intuitive but different values apply at
different stages in our evolution so it would be totally wrong for
example for Jesus to kill somebody because his dharmic path is
entirely different, and the same for Ghandi, with his principles of
ahimsa, violence of any sort would be wrong because his dharma

requires him to do things in different way, but for sincere and dutiful soldier it is the path he must follow and it is perfectly in harmony with the laws of nature.

You mentioned ahimsa and it is something that is not correctly understood and many people think that good behaviour will be rewarded by a sort of law of nature or by their God giving them a good school report so they smile at everyone and put on expression of pious goodwill, and force themselves not to do anything that will displease their God or earn bad karma.

True ahimsa however is something different, it is the absence of the desire to cause harm, it is peace that comes from deep within and it is the result, not the cause. It is the product of the deeper part of a mind that is at peace with itself, a mind without ego and it is like that because years of spiritual practices such as yoga and meditation have dissolved the negative tendencies, the tension, the inner conflicts, the fears we all have but are not aware of, and it is at peace with itself so it is at peace with the world around it and with the universe; that is true ahimsa.

You can sometimes see this in people you meet because they will have a sense of peace about them and you will instinctively know they are at peace. Play-acting simply will not help; cultivating an attitude or an image is not effective, it is just surface-level imitation, and you sometimes meet a person who smiles sweetly, who says nice things, and may even claim to be pacifist, but that is not ahimsa.

So it is no good putting on a big smile and telling everyone, including yourself, that you are peace-loving person because it will not earn you rewards of any sort and it will just add to the stress. You may fool your neighbours, you may even fool yourself but you cannot fool the laws of nature because you are just play-acting. No, it is what lies deep within you that counts.

True ahimsa is not an intellectual position, it cannot be presented like an actor presents his lines and it has to come from deep within because it is the result of spiritual attainment, not a means to achieve it. The mistake the Buddhists make in my opinion is that they confuse cause with effect, meaning they think that if they behave in a placid manner and if they consistently cultivate a peaceful demeanour this will somehow result in their spiritual growth and eventual enlightenment but in reality it is the other way around: if they endeavour to become more enlightened, for example by practicing meditation, they will find that they naturally and spontaneously attain state of ahimsa so their peace then comes from within, and so is unshakeable.

I found this all a bit confusing and contradictory. In Dr Moody's book Life After Life, one of the people who had experienced an NDE claims she learnt that to take a life, whether one's own or somebody else's, was to prevent that soul from evolving, and so was totally against the laws of nature. Yet the Bhagavad Gita, to the limited extent that I understand it, implies that it is not a universal rule, and this is what Dr Ramana suggests in the first part of his letter. If a soldier is on his dharmic path, then to kill someone, if no other option is available, is apparently acceptable. Because it is a dharmic action, there should be no karmic consequences.

I think the answer again lies in understanding the true workings of karma. In an earlier letter Dr Ramana had claimed that it is the thought process, the intention, behind the action that creates the karma. So if I were to kill someone because I hate them and want to inflict suffering upon them, then those thoughts would precipitate an adverse karmic response. But a soldier who is diligently fighting to defend his country is in a wholly different position. He does not specifically hate his enemy, in fact he would much prefer that the enemy turned around and went home, but the enemy obliges him to fight. The soldier thus has little or no choice if he wants to defend his family or nation. This soldier does not harbour enmity or hatred; he is not filled with satisfaction at the thought of killing someone.

For a karmic act to be fully effective, for good or for bad, it has to be 'complete,' meaning there must be a sequence of intention, action and reflection. Reflection can consist of either regret or satisfaction. If a soldier genuinely feels regret over having killed someone, and recognises the gravity of what he has done, the karmic outcome will be much less severe. But if he delights in killing, if he is indifferent, or if he uses it for self-glorification, then his motives must be regarded as negative and he must accept the karmic consequences.

Some soldiers, fanatical Nazis for example, were clearly not acting in self defence and often delighted in murderous behaviour. At the very least they were indifferent to the suffering they were causing. They thus have to accept the karmic response that their attitude produced. But a responsible soldier who is defending his nation, which in this context can be likened to an extended family, is performing action in accordance with his dharma. He did not join the military because he wanted to inflict suffering, so he is acting without hatred.

This is indeed borne out by the facts. Evidence shows that most soldiers are not proud of the fact that they have killed someone. They invariably regret it enormously and only killed because it was absolutely necessary. They often suffer from psychological distress later, perhaps feeling that they have somehow contravened a law of nature.

A surprisingly large proportion of soldiers simply won't shoot when required to. Brigadier General Samuel Marshal, the US Army's chief combat historian, did research on this subject during the Second World War, in Korea and in Vietnam. He interviewed thousands of combat veterans and found a common theme. He wrote, 'Fear of killing, rather than fear of being killed (was) the most common cause of battle failure.' In his book 'Men Against Fire' he claimed that in the Second World War 75% of combat troops never fired their personal weapons at the enemy for the purpose of killing, even though they were engaged in combat and under direct threat.

While there are some soldiers who kill only reluctantly, there are clearly those who do so with alacrity. The Nazis, Pol Pot's henchmen and Stalin's eager executioners all fall into this category. Their motives, the intentions before the act and the response afterwards, will ensure they reap their karmic dues. Those who kill reluctantly, out of duty, those who did not set out with hateful motives will not, according to Dr Ramana, suffer as a result.

Dear Dr Ramana

I think I have now got a picture, albeit a simplistic one, of the concept of dharma. But a part of it still puzzles me. In an earlier letter (the one where you gave the example of a dysfunctional family and described the interaction of the family members) you said that the wife chose *to be with her husband, and the daughter subsequently* chose *to be with these parents. Choice! Free will!*

Karma, as we have often discussed, is a deterministic force, in the sense that our destiny is forged in the mental attributes we each held at an earlier time. But the wife and the daughter are apparently making choices here, presumably before they are born. Their life situation was not in fact decided by their karma. How does this happen? Is there a clear distinction between karma and dharma in that karma is deterministic and dharma is the application of free will?

With best wishes, David

Dear David

Your question is an interesting one and has caused me much puzzlementation and concern so I discussed it with my father too, who is ancient Brahmin and also deaf who in fact only confuse matter furthermore for me.

Is dharma a matter of free will? My example of bird building its nest would suggest that it is not, as the bird has not made a conscious choice and is in a sense compelled to build nest at that time in a given way because that is law of nature which is embedded in the bird's DNA, so it is not doing it out of free will. But the decisions of the wife and daughter are different matter and lead me to think that bird nest was not good example to tell.

You are asking big and important question and I think the best thing is refer you to the work of Dr Michael Newton, who is regression hypnotist who has made big effort to understand the events that occur in periods between consecutive lives and uses a technique he has developed called Superconscious Hypnosis which helps people understand their life situation in terms of their relationships, based on the things they learned during the time between consecutive lives. I personally find his work honest and valid because of the consistency of descriptions given by his clients whilst under hypnosis, so it may not be empirically verifiable in the way Dr Stevenson's work is but the consistent reports he establishes suggests this sort of knowledge is reliable.

Dr Newton's clients describe the procedure a person undergoes before birth into new life on earth and how that person gets guidance from higher beings who help him decide which lessons he should learn in the life ahead and help him choose circumstances especially parents as they have profound influence as all parents do on the development of the life ahead, so that the problems that are faced on earth are ideally suited to the lessons that need to be learned.

So in this way a person who has difficult childhood such as the one in my earlier example will have decided before he is born that a troubled childhood will provide later opportunity to learn what is important and to develop as a soul and to increase understanding and qualities such as compassion, indeed a person who does not face difficulties in this life often does not learn important lessons. Or a person may choose to be born into poverty in order to learn about kindness, sharing or humility, or into a war zone to understand cruelty or compassion or to help others in that difficult situation.

It is therefore pointless to bemoan our circumstances in this life because they are of our own choosing, either by pre-birth choices we made or by our karmic bank balance. Also, this shows that suicide is utterly pointless because the tasks you have to face, whether karmic or through pre-birth choices, will remain whether you die or not, so if you do not resolve these tasks they will remain until a further time, but also you will have additional karmic burden due to amount of suffering you have caused to those around you by your suicide.

So to answer your question our life circumstances are not solely under the deterministic influence of karma, but there are also choices that we have each made to allow ourselves the best opportunity for growth so free will is also a factor, but it is a free will at a time before our birth.

Yours sincerely, K Ramana.

Dr Michael Newton, I soon discovered, differs from Dr Brian Weiss, mentioned earlier, in that his work focuses not on past lives specifically, but on the period between each of those lives. This phase includes reviewing our spiritual progress, learning and evaluating ideas with the assistance of more advanced souls, and making plans prior to a new earthly life. Dr Newton also helps clients to make connections between others who play a significant role in this life and their role in previous lives. As Dr Ramana states, the work is hallmarked by a consistency and professionalism that is hard to dispute.

Dr Newton's first book, 'Journey of Souls' was based on his experience of over 20 years of research, during which time he had induced hypnotic regression in over 7000 clients. What convinced him of the validity of this knowledge was the sheer consistency of the descriptions that clients related to him, irrespective of their culture, nationality or religious views. Many other practitioners have seen the same consistency with their clients, thus achieving the scientific test of duplication.

Dr Newton was quite atheistic in his approach to begin with, to the point of being somewhat dismissive of spiritual matters. But experience with two of his patients gave him a different perspective. One of these patients came to him complaining of a sharp pain in his side that conventional medicine could not account for. Dr Newton hypnotised his client and took him back to his childhood, expecting to discover some long-forgotten injury. Nothing became apparent. So he asked the client to go back to the source of the pain. To Dr Newton's surprise the patient began describing his part in a First World War battle, where he lay dying of a bayonet injury. Dr Newton asked him to describe his circumstances, his battalion, the location, his uniform insignia and so on. All of this was consistent with historical fact. He realised that here was an area of knowledge that could be helpful to many of his clients. Then another client took Dr Newton even further into this new arena. This lady told him about her sense of profound loneliness and how she felt lost, alienated and unable to relate to others. Under hypnosis she began to describe her life in another realm, between her lives on this earth. She told of her spiritual friends and said how much she missed them.

As a result of these two experiences Dr Newton gradually began to focus on the period between our incarnations. He discovered that some of us are new to this world and therefore have little to show in the way of wisdom or spiritual under-standing. Others are 'old souls,' people who have been here before and are beginning to recognise patterns and establish values. These 'old souls' are often characterised by a willingness to help others and a desire to increase their understanding. They are usually unassuming people who shun the noisy fripperies of the lives of 'new souls' and have a greater degree of insight and intuition. Most people are somewhere in between – each of us learning lessons, each working out our karma according to the experiences and events of earlier lives.

Dr Newton realised that we evolve in soul-groups, made up of people who are close to us and who are at a similar level of evolution. Prior to each new life we plan our future, choosing our circumstances and parents to give us the opportunities to learn new lessons and resolve issues that we have been unable to settle before. Someone close to us, perhaps a member of our soul group, may choose to accompany us, to help us and also to learn their own lessons. Before birth the person then has various discussions with what could be described as a 'Council of Wise Men,' sometimes referred to as 'The Lords of Karma.' These are highly evolved beings who have much greater wisdom and can offer guidance as to which lessons and experiences would be most beneficial to our evolution. For example, if a person has caused pain and distress in an earlier life, such as by committing a murder, the new life must in some way compensate for that act, to balance the karma. The person cannot evolve any further until they fully understand and appreciate the distress they have caused to others. So their next life may have to include experiences of a similar nature, such as witnessing the murder of someone close to them. This is not a punishment as such; it is done out of choice and is a means for our compassion and understanding to grow.

Once we are in our new life we apparently experience a form of amnesia. Interestingly, this amnesia does not become fully effective until we are about 5 or 6 years old, which explains why some children have memories of earlier lives, as described by Dr Stevenson.

We are here to learn, to sort out our issues in an innocent way, a way that is entirely of our own making. If we were to retain memories of our earlier lives and our between-lives states we would only be performing our actions according to a set of earlier-learned rules, so we would not be obliged to figure things out for ourselves and thus truly learn those lessons. This in fact demonstrates why dogma and blind faith are inadequate as spiritual paths; they obstruct the process of investigation and personal endeavour.

At the end of that particular life we return to the spiritual realm and are welcomed by our loved-ones. We find ourselves in a state of sublime happiness and serenity; the travails of our earthly life are over and we can take time to look back and see clearly how we responded to our life's challenges. Everything is evaluated in terms of love and non-violence. Even if we have behaved badly we still experience a sense of bliss, albeit tinged with the regret at having hurt others. The 'Lords of Karma' and our own personal spirit guide help us through this evaluative process, and help us to decide which lessons require further work. There is nothing in Dr Newton's descriptions that suggests punishment, a hell or any form of judgement; we simply observe ourselves and see clearly where we have been lacking. We keep coming back to a life in this world until we achieve a full understanding.

Chapter 14

Ancient Wisdom

I was to discover that much is written about karma in ancient eastern scriptures; it is a philosophy that is more or less uniformly accepted. However, my personal view is that these writings are not always helpful. There are numerous schools of thought and they are sometimes inconsistent and not very rigorous in their argument. They are open to misinterpretation. They have been re-translated many times and the original meaning may have been lost or distorted. After all, a person can only translate a text according to his own level of understanding, which may in some cases have been limited. Also, we know little about the cultural circumstances of those times, and it can be misleading to look at an idea outside of its social setting. Some early texts may in fact have been lost, as accidents of history, so we cannot be sure we are getting the full picture.

We have to respect these books but we also have to be careful not to venerate them just because they are old. We can easily fall into the trap of inductive reasoning: some ancient philosophies are valuable; this is an ancient philosophy, therefore it must be valuable. Some may indeed be valuable but some may also be misleading or mistaken, so we ultimately have to rely on our own discrimination.

As Westerners we like to dissect ideas, separate them into their component parts, then analyse them. This is not always possible with oriental philosophies such as karma as they are very much holistic systems, and specific aspects are often embedded in the scriptures as a whole.

The task of evaluation is made more complicated by the fact that there are dozens of different schools and sub-schools within each of the main eastern religions. The term *Hindu* for example covers a plethora of theology, myths, art, dogma, scriptures, culture and rituals, all brought together over thousands of years. In fact the word *Hindu* was introduced by the British. The Indians did not give their philosophy a specific name; it was simply regarded as the universal laws of nature. It is perhaps a Western habit to regard spiritual matters as a separate task, distinct from our daily activities.

The concepts that eastern religions contain have to be understood by a wide range of people, of varying ability and education, so some of it is obscure and challenging, some is less esoteric. There is something in Hinduism and Buddhism for everyone, so they have evolved into numerous sects and schools. Things are complicated even more by the use of different terms to describe concepts; there are no standardised definitions.

In earlier times the philosophy of karma was often adopted as a convenient political tool to maintain the status quo and to justify India's caste system. A prince, for example, would extol the concept of karma as a way of justifying his current situation, claiming that it was brought about by his virtue in an earlier life and he was therefore fully deserving of his wealth and position in society. An underprivileged Dalit, an Untouchable, on the other hand, only had himself to blame for his lowly status, as again it reflected his karma. In this way the ruling classes managed to control social mobility and keep everyone firmly in their allotted place. (In this respect they made the flawed assumption that it is a spiritual benefit to be born into royalty. A cursory glance at history in fact shows us just the opposite: that princes and princesses are frequently unhappy, selfish and somewhat vulgar, and on an evolutionary path to nowhere.) In a similar way, karma has often been used as an excuse to subjugate women.

The earliest texts that form a spiritual philosophy are the Vedas; they are in fact the earliest recorded writing in history, dating from somewhere around 1500 to 1000 BCE. The word

Veda simply means knowledge; it does not denote a religion as such, though many religions were subsequently based upon Vedic ideas. There were initially four Vedas, the principal one being Rig Veda, followed by Yajur Veda, Sama Veda and Atharva Veda; they are collectively referred to as the Samhitas. Later Vedas consist of the Brahmanas, Aranyakas, Upanishads and Vedangas; these works formed the basis of the Brahmanical tradition.

The four original Vedas consist largely of mantras, hymns, spells and incantations. According to tradition they were 'cognised' by enlightened sages whilst in deep meditation. They were eventually written down in Sanskrit, a language in which there is a close vibrational affinity between the sound of a word and the subject it relates to. This is a concept known as Nama Rupa, or name and form, and is an important factor in the understanding of mantras, religious music and chanting. To this day, Brahmins will spend many years learning to recite large parts of the Vedas, with particular attention being paid to precise pronunciation.

It is often assumed that, because the Vedas are such foundational pieces of Indian literature, and because karma and reincarnation are fundamental to Indian ontology, these concepts must have been first elucidated in the early Vedas. In fact the Vedas do not say anything about them; ideas of reincarnation and karma didn't appear until some 500 years later. The early Jain and Buddhist literature were the first to express these ideas, as part of a separate culture known as Greater Magadha, located in the eastern Ganges plain near what is now known as Patna. It was quite different to the Vedic culture to the west and gave rise to the Jain and Buddhist traditions, both of whom nurtured the twin philosophies of reincarnation and karma. The Magadha influence spread rapidly to the Vedic areas of India and, after initial resistance on the part of the Brahmins, these ideas were soon adopted by the numerous Vedic schools of thought. This synthesis formed the basis of what is now known as Hinduism. It must be said that not all historians agree on this matter, many claiming that karma and reincarnation were in fact Brahmanical ideas.

One of the principal aspects of Hinduism is Vedanta, which loosely translated means 'beyond the Vedas.' The term Vedanta describes a group of philosophical traditions, Advaita, Vishishtadvaita and Dvaita, devoted to the understanding of self-realisation or personal evolution. Vedanta is not entirely based upon one teacher or one specific book, although it principally refers to the Upanishads and the Bhagavad Gita. At its heart Vedanta sees the universe as a seamless, unified whole which is a manifestation of a Supreme Consciousness, known as Brahman. Each of us as individuals are not in fact individuals at all but an intrinsic, inseparable part of that whole; our consciousness is part of the total consciousness. And the reality we see around us, the material world, is a field of vibrating energy that is an outward manifestation or expression of that totality.

Vedanta in general holds that although karma is an impersonal law of nature it is not completely independent; it is subject to the influence of a supreme God who metes out happiness or suffering according to our needs.

An important branch of Vedanta is Advaita, which is inscribed in various books including the Upanishads and The Brahma Sutras, a scripture attributed to Badaryana. The Advaitist philosophy as a whole was brought together by Adi Shankara, whose writings are seen as crucial to its development. Advaita is principally concerned with the identity of Atman, our individual higher self, and how to enhance its relationship with Brahman, so Shankara thus puts forward a non-dualistic view of reality. Advaita describes karma as an unseen metaphysical force which cannot decide in itself what an appropriate karmic response should be; thus a personal God is again required.

The Bhagavad Gita is a significant part of the Advaita Vedanta tradition and has a lot to say about how we are reborn. The 'Gita,' as it is often referred to, is attributed to a learned sage called Veda Vyasa, and its 700 verses form part of the Mahabarata, one of the major scriptures in Indian religious literature. The Gita describes the dialogue between Lord Krishna and a warrior prince called Arjuna, which takes place on a battlefield, an allegory representing our day to day lives.

In Chapter 7 it states that the thoughts we have at the moment of death largely determine the life we will be reborn into, so a dying person should focus on a god or spiritual ideal. I personally find this difficult to accept. A person may lead a blameless and dutiful life, then meet their death in the jaws of a hungry tiger. That person's last thoughts will, understandably, be about tigers. Does that dictate a future lifetime as *panthera tigris*? One would hope not. I suspect however that something slightly different is meant, not just specific thoughts about tigers or the immediate circumstances. The Gita is perhaps referring to the underlying demeanour of the dying person, such as peacefulness, goodwill or acceptance, and it is these qualities that contribute to a good rebirth.

There are many other schools within the Hindu philosophical tradition. The Samkya school is one of the oldest. It sees karma as an impersonal law of nature but proposes that highly evolved beings in another realm administer everything on God's behalf; they are sometimes referred to as Devas (beings of light) or what Westerners would refer to as angels. The Shaivanist school is similar in that a God is required because karma cannot identify the specific individual that it must deliver its fruits to. Followers of Shaivanism claim that all souls somehow gravitate to particular mortal bodies during certain cycles of creation, and it uses karma as a justification of the Indian caste system. The Mimansa philosophy, contained within the Jaimini Sutras, is essentially atheistic in regard to karma. A personal God, it is claimed, is unnecessary, as karma is a self-contained law of cause and effect so has no need of outside intervention. But they allow that it can be influenced by rituals, such as fire ceremonies (yagyas).

Buddhism also has a multitude of schools and sects. The Buddhists love to systematise their knowledge; they categorise ideas and put them into lists. It's as if they want their concepts neatly stored in a filing cabinet so that they can quickly lay their hands on an explanation for any given situation. Every idea is intellectualised, numbered and ordered; thus there are Three Marks of Existence, Four Noble Truths, Five Aggregates, The Noble Eightfold Path, The Twelve Nidanas and so on. If you ever need an office manager, get a Buddhist.

The reason for this structured approach is that early Buddhist teachings, like many others of the time, were handed down verbally, by way of sutras. Sutras are short, terse sentences that monks would learn by heart. When the monks subsequently imparted these ideas to their own students the sutra would be expanded and elaborated upon, thus ensuring that the teaching was passed on in a consistent way.

It would be difficult to summarise Buddhist thought in just a few lines as its complexities and profundities can take a lifetime of study to fully understand. But the foundation of Buddhist philosophy is contained within 'The Four Noble Truths.' These tell us that life involves suffering and that we can avoid or mitigate this suffering if we create a shift in our consciousness or perception. Thus we must examine and understand our state of mind, our inner self. Buddhism then elucidates various practical means for achieving these inner changes; this is known as 'The Noble Eightfold Path' and it forms the essence of a Buddhist's day-to-day practice. They are Right Understanding, Right Thought, Right Speech, Right Action, Right Livelihood, Right Effort, Right Mindfulness and finally Right Meditation.

Buddhism differs from Vedanta in one important respect. Vedantic philosophy holds meditation (specifically the deeper, more tranquil state of mind known as Samadhi) to be the key to our spiritual unfoldment. The other qualities, such as Right Understanding, are in a sense almost by-products of Samadhi and these qualities will occur spontaneously and effortlessly if we meditate regularly and thus dissolve our inner stresses. Trying to establish Right Understanding consciously or intellectually will not help us very much as that would be a surface-level activity so does not counter the influence of the deeper, more transcendent aspects of our mind. Only meditation can do that. So, according to Vedanta, Buddhists are confusing cause with effect; the qualities enumerated in The Noble Eightfold Path are in fact the *results* of exposure to Samadhi, not the causes of it. Buddhists, however, would claim that by adopting The Noble Eightfold Path as a way of life we suffuse our being with a different perspective; this will eventually translate into a more fulfilling and evolutionary state of mind and help us on our path to enlightenment.

Karma is an important aspect of Buddhism, and is regarded as the force that drives *samsara*, the continuing cycle of birth, death and rebirth. In the Theravada school karma is seen as a purely mechanical process of cause and effect. There is no possibility of divine intervention or mitigation; karma is simply a law of nature. Some texts of the Mahayana and Vajrayana schools claim that reciting mantras or religious passages can relieve the effects of negative karma, although Buddha himself denied that anyone can avoid their karmic dues once a deed has been committed. Buddha also said that karma is the factor determining how we are reborn, thus karma is often mentioned alongside the idea of reincarnation. The Japanese Tendai school claims however that Amida Buddha has the power to override the karmic influence that traps a person in the cycle of samsara. Amida is the Japanese term for the personification of the truth that suffuses all of us; it is what other Buddhists may call dharma, or universal truth.

Tantric Buddhism has been described as the means to accelerate our personal growth by rapidly neutralising all existing karma, a process known by the delightful name of *sarvanasthi-takarmabhedavidhana*, (and no, I didn't make that up, despite it containing my forename). This is a system of rituals and meditation, with a heavy reliance on one's guru.

The Tibetan Book of the Dead, or Bardo Thodal, is a text by the great Tibetan Buddhist teacher Padmasambhava, and is devoted to the process of dying. It describes in detail the journey that we must all make after death. It does not talk specifically about karma in the conventional sense, although its aim is to help people recognise their own true nature. It urges us not to be afraid of anything in the afterlife, neither judgement, apparition nor deity, as these are all simply projections of our own consciousness. Advice is also given on how to achieve a good birth in the next life.

All schools of Buddhism are quite clear that it is the intention, not the act, that causes the karmic response. The actual act is a result of the intention, so there is no direct causal link between the act in itself and the eventual karmic outcome.

Some modern Buddhists see karma as something of an embarrassment. In these politically correct times there are concerns over the idea that someone's physical handicaps, social class, race and level of wealth can be explained, perhaps dismissively, as a result of past actions. They conjecture that there would be no point in working towards, for example, greater social equality if an immutable law of nature is what determines a person's status in the first place. This is a sensitive issue, but the response seems to be that karma is not the same as destiny; karma allows for free will, which bestows some personal control over our future circumstances and how we deal with them. Karma lays the groundwork for a person's life, but free will allows personal choices to be made, which can modify or mitigate the circumstances, especially in the future. The karmic explanation does not in any way relieve us of the obligation to be compassionate towards those in an unenviable situation.

Taoists always inspire an affection in me. They are tolerant and wise, and I fondly imagine that they have some special knowledge, some inestimable secret held only by themselves, which they can't be troubled to tell anyone else about. They quaintly refer to the manifest field of life as 'The Ten Thousand Things.'

The word Tao means The Way, referring to the unseen laws of nature, the ultimate source or all-pervading principle that gives birth to everything. The concept has existed in China for thousands of years, but was first written down by Lao Tse, a librarian in the Chou Imperial Court, in a book called Tao Te Ching or The Book of Tao. Lao Tse quietly observed the vulgar and egotistical goings-on in the royal court until one day he tiredly announced: 'I really am *disgusted* with you all,' and disappeared into the sunset on the back of a water buffalo. He was never seen again.

Taoist writings say little about karma. What they do say suggests a Buddhist view, but mention is made of spirits who monitor our behaviour and reduce or increase our lifespan accordingly. They also refer to astrology, claiming that 'evil stars' send down calamities on those who transgress natural law.

Karma is an intrinsic and important aspect of Jainism, and much is written about it in their scriptures. The second century Jain text Bhagavati Aradhana says, 'There is nothing mightier in the world than karma; karma tramples down all power.' The Jains hold that karma dictates the circumstances of our next birth. The influence of a supreme God, or indeed lesser gods, cannot alter that outcome; it is entirely a matter of natural law, though we can mitigate the effects to some extent by performing austerities and modifying our personal behaviour, for which purpose we have free will.

Depending on the moral choices we have made we may

reincarnate in a heaven or a hell, or as humans or animals. There is an innate moral order within and throughout the cosmos, so these choices are vitally important; they allow us to live in harmony with that cosmic order, which leads to the decrease and ultimately the eradication of karmic influences. Jainism is characterised by austerity, absolute integrity, and the need for penances as a way towards spiritual growth. The concept of *ahimsa* predominates Jain thought.

Jains use the analogy of gold ore to describe karma, which is symbolic of the unrefined state of our original soul. The gold is in there somewhere, buried and hidden amongst a mass of worthless mineral dross. Only by refining the ore and throwing away the dross can we find the gold. The dross represents our individual karmic burden, which pollutes and obscures our real self – the gold. When we are rid of the dross we attain Moksha (enlightenment) which is regarded as the liberation from the bondage of karma.

How do we remove the dross? According to the Jain canon, The Bhagvati Sutras, we can only do so by following a path of purification, which consists of pure thinking and austerities. God has no impact upon one's progress towards Moksha; it is solely the responsibility of the individual. Behaviour plays a vitally important part: the killing of animals puts one on the path to hell, and dishonesty leads to rebirth as an animal. Keeping promises and performing austerities leads us towards Moksha, while humility and compassion ensure birth into a good family.

Jains have given a lot of thought as to how karma works. They suggest that it exists as a minute substance, perhaps what we today would call sub-atomic particles, which permeates, indeed pollutes, our physical body. These are called *dravya karma* and they reside in each person in an interactive field called *karmana sanra*. (This is similar to what Vedantists and others would call akasha, although akasha is universal, not limited to the individual). The particles 'colour' the body, according to the quality of the karma. The colours, called *Leysa,* are symbolically blue, black and grey, which are inauspicious and result in calamities and misfortune, and yellow, white and red, which bring varying degrees of good fortune. When we have achieved sufficient purification these colours fade and ultimately disappear and so we do not need to reincarnate again.

Curiously, the Jains place importance on the action attached to karma as well as the intention behind it. So if I cause suffering unintentionally, for example in a road traffic accident, I will reap negative karma. This is contrary to the Buddhist position, where intention is paramount. The Jains' view is that the accident was my karmic responsibility because it was my carelessness that caused it; I should not have put myself in the position where I could harm others.

Of all the world's creeds, Jainism seems to place the greatest importance on karma and the understanding of it. Their theory of karma puts responsibility for our fortunes or misfortunes squarely on to our own shoulders, but they also believe in free will, which allows us to mitigate any ill fortune and determine our own future.

Chapter 15

The Laws of Nature

I hadn't heard from Dr Ramana for some time. I always looked forward to receiving his letters; they gave me a novel perspective on life and made me think about things in a different way. I had collected a few books on Eastern philosophy by now and though I didn't study them diligently I enjoyed thumbing through them and picking up fresh ideas.

One of the most valuable aspects of an understanding of karma, however limited that understanding may be, is that it offers some sort of explanation as to the iniquities and injustices in life. This has to be treated with some caution; if an idea is too attractive, too convenient, it can easily become an emotional comforter and our scepticism and reason may be subjugated to our personal needs. But a critical understanding of karma is invaluable; it may show us a picture of life without random unfairness and explain why things are the way they are.

So I asked Dr Ramana a very simple question: Why do bad things happen to good people?

Firstly, (he replied), let's look at this word 'bad.' and ask is there such a concept as 'bad' in an objective sense or is it just something we humans have concocted with our limited view of the world? Take bad weather, for example. Can weather really be 'bad'? It may not suit us; it may be inconvenient, but perhaps badness is just a label we apply because it seems bad from our small, selfish view of the world, when in fact the weather is a marvellous phenomenon being a huge and intricate display of numerous laws of nature but we are so wrapped up in our ego-needs (we're scared that rain may damage our nice clothes) that we miss the grandeur and beauty of it.

Let me give you better example. The other day I dropped a bottle

*of fruit juice as I was taking it from the fridge and my 'small-self'
response was to be irritated because I was already late for work and
now I had a mess to clear up, but think about it for a moment: the
bottle, as it fell, described a precise arc through the air, an arc that
could be expressed in exact mathematical terms, then it hit the floor
and broke up in a perfect display of nature's laws as the impact
caused the glass to fracture in a precise way taking the path of least
resistance, then the fragments flew through the air in another series
of perfect arcs, and the juice flowed briefly but perfectly along the
floor and began to dry, again in accordance with more laws.*

*Because I was already slightly stressed due to my lateness I
failed totally to see any beauty in this event and it was just a
nuisance so I grumbled and sighed and thought only about myself
and my frivolous ego-needs and thus I missed the elegance of this
tiny but divine ballet.*

*Now I suspect you mean 'bad' in a much more serious context
than bottles falling onto floors. Some people suffer enormously and
it often seems without reason, like the people who get caught up in
wars for example and appear to suffer through no fault of their own,
and children who are often innocent victims, but perhaps we would
see a larger picture if our horizons were not so limited and maybe,
like the falling bottle, we would see that there is a beautiful yet
tragic playing-out of the laws of nature, above and beyond what we
normally see.*

*I want to tell you about some of my experiences with children, as
a doctor, because we see many children here at the hospital but let
me tell you about one case when a child was brought in with burns.
The mother was drunk and soon became hysterical and had to be
restrained and she has eight children with eight different fathers
plus she has a drug dependency and the children are destitute,
underfed and live in squalid conditions, but still she has more
children and still she beats them when they cry before drinking
herself into oblivion.*

So is there a broader view here? Is this incident also a playing out of natural law? We know from our discussion on Near Death Experiences that we are all put on this planet to do various things: to learn to love, and to try to understand our lives, our journey, ourselves, and we also know that Nature always gives us the opportunity to learn the things we need to learn.

So how can this sad unfortunate lady learn to love her sad unfortunate children? The answer is she simply cannot, not in this life; after all what could she do, read a book? Go to university? Ask a priest? Ask her friends? Of course not; what could anyone say to her?

We also see in the hospital the intense grief of parents when they lose a child. Just last week a boy of six was brought in and we were unable to save him and the parents were devastated as you would expect, and this happens many times; it is a part of my job yet it always disturbs me and I always wish I could offer the parents an explanation, but I cannot.

Now let me change the subject for a moment. Imagine a sheet of paper with a dozen numbers printed on it and as a layman you may look at all these numbers and they would appear as random, but a mathematician may look at these same numbers and see a pattern, for example he would realise that they are all prime numbers, or multiples of 13 or something like that, because his enhanced awareness, his greater knowledge, would allow him to perceive a pattern where others do not.

So, what patterns would we see if our perception was widened and enhanced? We see people behaving recklessly with other people's lives, children's lives, and we know that these people have to learn to act differently, act with love and we know from our discussion on Pragya Parad (mistake of the intellect) that conventional learning will not help as it has huge limitations, and we see parents losing a child in an apparently random way, all of which makes us ask: is there a connection?

Maybe the parents I mentioned and their apparently tragic loss of a child is in fact a playing-out of the laws of nature, a precisely choreographed dance to the music of time, an event that is neither good nor bad, but instead a lesson to be worked through. To our eyes each death is a tragedy, but perhaps the people caught up in it are learning a lesson that they are obliged to learn, so maybe one day the lady with the drug problem will be obliged to learn lessons that are so clearly escaping her in this present life and she will only learn those lessons by experiencing appropriate events so she may perhaps love a child then lose that child and in that way she may eventually come to understand the value of a child's life. This is why karmic results are delayed, maybe for lifetimes; the right circumstances have to be in position for the relevant lesson to take place.

Each death is a tragedy, but it is also the playing-out of the laws of nature, and in that respect it is like a divine ballet, an inevitable, entrancing yet sometimes grotesque enactment of the laws of karma.

I hope this will give you some food of thinking and will explain perhaps why bad things happen to good people and vice versa.

Yours sincerely, K Ramana

A few days after I'd received Dr Ramana's letter a newspaper article caught my eye. It was about a woman who had been arrested in the USA. She had been an SS officer at a Nazi concentration camp in 1944. She had apparently stood at the front of the queue as people, Jews mainly, disembarked from the trains of death. This woman hated children. When she saw a baby she would wrench it from the mother's arms and trample it to death. She would jump up and down, crushing every tiny bone in its wretched body. Sometimes she would grab an infant by the ankles and smash it against a wall. The tiny pathetic body – frequently they were not quite dead – would be thrown onto a truck and taken to a burnpit.

That was as near to an image of hell as I could ever imagine. This awful woman was beyond feeling, totally desensitized by her own hatred. What could one say to such a person? What could one ever do to persuade her to change that mind set?

Nothing. A prison sentence would only harden her heart even further; nothing would ever penetrate that level of inhumanity. She could only learn, I supposed, by suffering herself, by loving a child then losing it. In that way she would feel, comprehend, know, another person's pain. She would learn to value love.

I have known two couples who have lost children. In both cases they were good, sensible parents; in no way could they be described as un-loving or in any way heartless, indifferent or irresponsible. Their loss seemed cruel, random and undeserving. I am absolutely sure that in this life they had never done anything to cause suffering to a child. But what of earlier lives? What about another life, in an earlier epoch, when cruelty was the norm, an everyday occurrence, when children were hung with a rope for petty crimes. And what about our own dark ages, the twentieth century, when children were gassed for simply being born Jewish?

We do not know what happened to us in an earlier incarnation. We do not know what we did, how we behaved and what lessons we are here to learn. One thing is certain: those parents who lost children will have, through such tragic events, become aware of human suffering, their own, and of course their children's. Maybe now they are better for that, more compassionate, more dutiful, more patient. If they can learn from their tragedy, if they can widen their awareness, they may see that it could all be part of their growth. This is not to dismiss their suffering with a glib, simplistic theory. It does not diminish anyone's pain. But if it takes away some of the sense of futility, the feeling of random, meaningless suffering, then it may make the loss easier to bear. We may no longer hold our head in our hands and ask why. And if each of us can see, feel, a semblance of truth in it, we will have taken a step forward in our spiritual evolution.

But what is fascinating, to the point of being bizarre, is that, to Dr Ramana, all of this suffering, all of these tragedies, are in a sense not bad – that was my original question – but natural, value free and imbued with inevitability. And paradoxically they have within them, if we can but see it, a hideous yet celestial form of beauty.

Chapter 16

Karma and War

Dear Dr Ramana

As you will have no doubt heard, the United Kingdom and a number of other countries have recently seen fit to invade Iraq. This has caused consternation amongst the public here, as many are implacably opposed to war. My wife and I are acutely aware of the situation as my wife's cousin Mark is in the army and has just been flown out to the war zone.

I am not sure how to view this situation. Years ago I was enthusiastic in my opposition to the Vietnam war and indeed attended many anti-war demonstrations. Now I see things in a less black-and-white way, which is a side effect of getting older I suppose! We are (allegedly) at risk of weapons of mass destruction, so in that respect we have every right to defend ourselves. Also, the Iraqi regime is a tyranny, so the world will be a safer place if and when it is removed.

But on the other side of the argument stands the horror of war, the inevitable suffering and destruction, the grief and deprivation, and that surely is wrong. Tens of thousands of innocent people, including children, will be caught up in it through no fault of their own.

Is it all simply the laws of karma coming into play? I would appreciate your point of view.

With best wishes, David

Dear David

Yes of course I am aware of the tragic events unfolding in the Middle East, and these things are of course not easy to understand so I cannot give you simple straightforward answer to this question: how to respond to such things, although I wish I could.

I have perhaps various ways to look at it, the first being dharma because as I have told you a soldier has duty to protect others providing he does not act with hatred or negative thought like revenge, but this is not easy as battle and circumstances are stressful and traumatic so soldier can easily succumb to anger and behave in improper way, and this of course is karmic detriment. But this is complex argument and there is danger in oversimplification and trying to get one theory to fit all circumstances because each event is different and depends on the motive and mental attitude of the soldier concerned.

Of course there will be many people involved in this war who are working out their karma as they each have their own lessons to learn and debts to pay and also their family at home maybe have to undergo grief because of their own karma and some will have made a conscious pre-birth choice to partake in it as they wish to learn and develop an understanding of human tragedy.

Other point of view is that this war is not caused by the conscious decisions that we hear about from world leaders. My belief is that the war was inevitable because it is the outcome or manifestation or expression of the collective thoughts of all the Iraqi people because for many years they have lived in great fear and hatred under a dictatorship and this continual fear and trauma creates negative influence in the minds of individuals, which inevitable outcome is war so if millions of people together think only fear and anger, that thought must find expression somewhere, which is of course karma, the expression of our thoughts, desires and intentions, so there cannot be peace unless each individual has peace within him.

There have always been wars, but when you look at social history you see that most of population always lived in fear, ignorance, superstition so the events that eventually surround them will display these qualities. An example if a bit extreme is the rise of Hitler in nineteen thirties because everyone had suffered trauma earlier in the first war, then there was deprivation, hyper-inflation and thus trauma in each of millions of individuals who were each to some degree traumatised, so it was inevitable that these collective powerful influences would result in tragedy, so the outcome was worst war in history.

And it was same for Soviet Union who had suffered years of purges and pogroms which meant whole population is collectively traumatised and so produce conflict, in the same way that a human body may produce negative responses such as cancer or other bad condition if hatred and trauma is continued for long time.

So the outward symptoms and reasons of this war, the weapons of mass destruction for example, and the speeches and policy decisions, are all in a sense only the surface symptoms, because the real causes are much more subtle and not understood by the political leaders or the military, and the real causes can only be addressed by creating peace in the individual and thus collectively, so the use of weapons is like pouring water onto the leaves of a thirsty tree instead of onto the roots which is the proper place because that is where the problem is, not at the leaves.

I hope this will give you something to think about and I hope your relative will come through this event safely.

Regards, K Ramana.

To Dr Ramana these events are apparently all part of nature's workings; it is people making choices, but on a huge scale as a group. His response wasn't resignation or despair; it wasn't a cold indifference. He could see that each suffering person was involved in their own journey, their own story, as part of a much larger, collective narrative. Everyone was partaking in the creation of a nation's history. Everything was working itself out, slowly, lifetime by lifetime, according to nature's laws and nature's intelligence.

He clearly states that there can never be world peace until there is peace within each individual. Philosophies, great plans of action, are clearly worthless; they are intellectual fripperies that ultimately achieve nothing and invariably cause suffering. As Dr Ramana once said, after thousands of years of thinking we still haven't solved any of the big issues.

Peace, or the lack of it, is apparently the responsibility of the individual. The history of the world can perhaps be seen as the huge landscape that we have all had a part in painting, or a vast choral work sung by a choir of seven billion. Those seven billion souls are all to some degree damaged; they are angry, disappointed or selfish at a very deep level. So the song we all create is devoid of harmony and full of restless discord. We are all part of that choir because, as quantum physics tells us, we are all part of a vast but subtle interconnected web. We mentally design the world we live in with our thoughts; we create our collective karma. Abstract philosophies and ideals are just words and will not help us, any more than it helps for an angry individual to put on a facade of peacefulness. Peace, in this perspective, cannot be achieved by intellectual means; it has to come from a level deep within us all.

How can that happen? How can we create a peaceful world? Well a phrase by Sri Patanjali, the father of yoga, may help us. He said: *Tat sannidhau vairatyagah,* which means, 'In the vicinity of a peaceful mind, hostile tendencies disappear.' To fully understand this we have to recognise that at a quantum level, mind, consciousness, is not localised. It is not restricted to the inside of our head; it is not a separate entity, existing in splendid isolation. It is instead a field, it is a part of an expanded, unified and interrelated intelligence that suffuses all of nature at its finest level.

Sri Patanjali's phrase does not mean that if you sit close to someone who is meditating you will feel peaceful, although that may in fact be true. It means that at a very subtle level of nature's functioning the meditator is exerting a peaceful influence on the collective consciousness of which he is a part. Experienced meditators can learn to use this phenomenon to exert an effect on the world outside of themselves. There are specific techniques to do this called Siddhis (the word simply means perfections) which are explained in Sri Patanjali's Yoga Sutras. Meditators can learn how to think specific thoughts at a deep, almost silent level.

This process has two interconnected effects: it accelerates the process of the cleaning out of all of the negative residue within the meditator's nervous system, and it has a subtle influence on the surrounding environment. Thoughts at this refined level permeate collective consciousness, and the deeper the level of the thoughts the more effective they are. It is rather like the song of a whale: at the ocean's surface the sound will only carry a short distance, but when the whale is hundreds of feet down the music can be heard and enjoyed over thousands of miles.

Practically speaking it would be impossible to achieve world peace by getting every single person on the planet to somehow resolve all their issues, dissolve all their stresses and be at peace with themselves. It would be great if we could do that, but realistically it is not going to happen. But according to Sri Patanjali that approach is not necessary; it just takes a small number of people to be at peace, in deep meditation, for the effect to permeate collective consciousness. Hostility, he says, ceases in the vicinity of a person at peace. The birth of an enemy simply does not occur.

Months passed without a letter from Dr Ramana. I wondered if he was still in good health, or indeed still alive, but I assumed one of his family would have informed me if anything was amiss. I had kept all of his letters in a blue lever-arch file, along with my transcriptions and replies. From time to time I would idly thumb through them and reflect on the things we'd discussed. It was now over 20 years since I had briefly met him, and I could not deny that I had learned a lot from him. I was different now, a different person, in a contented, easy sort of way.

Even so I sometimes envied the uncomplicated folk who simply got on with their lives, played games, bought things, believed what they were told to believe. But I knew I couldn't share that life any more. I saw it played out daily on the television, those distant, discarded values of mine, the adverts, the phoney actors, the facile music, egos by the dozen. I just didn't want that any more.Indeed, certain aspects of human behaviour now seemed quite bizarre. I would, for example, turn on the television to find grown men dressed up as cowboys, pretending to kill one another. It seemed pointless and slightly ridiculous. Another time, Sandy and I were out walking when we came across a cricket match being played on a village green. The men were throwing a ball and trying to hit it. They grew excited. They started shouting.

About that time I received a strange note from Dr Ramana. It simply said: *The only things worth collecting are thank-you letters.* There was a scrawl of a signature. It was written on the back of a postcard and had been placed in an envelope addressed by somebody else.

For the next few days the card sat above the fireplace. I would glance at it occasionally and look for some hidden meaning. It seemed enigmatically simple, given the hundreds of pages of complex Vedic knowledge that Dr Ramana had sent me over the years. Eventually it went into the folder, sitting on top of all the other letters, and I forgot about it.

Chapter 17

Collective Madness

Dear Dr Ramana

Your letter earlier this year regarding war and the causes of war was interesting and thought-provoking and has helped me to understand the Vedic view of this tragic situation. Sadly the circumstances in the Middle East have become all too real for us here. My wife's cousin Mark, who I mentioned in an earlier letter, was tragically killed in action last week. His body was flown home yesterday and we will attend the funeral next week.

My wife is very upset, naturally, and Mark's mother is distraught, having lost her husband only a year ago. We visited her a few days ago and both of us found it extremely distressing. Deaths of soldiers can so easily be reduced to statistics. It is only when you are confronted with the personal loss that you can fully appreciate the enormity of war.

I am trying to see this from a much bigger perspective but it is difficult when faced with the immediate circumstances. I am sure there is a karmic angle to this, but right now that seems to be overwhelmed by the actual events.

With best wishes, David

Mark's funeral took place a few days after I sent the letter. I found the service upsetting, even though I wasn't especially close to him. The vicar spoke about sacrifices, patriotism and pride, and I wanted to ask him what the hell he was talking about. A high ranking officer stood up and told us how well-liked Mark was and how proud he was to have served with him. He saluted Mark's coffin.

I found it all disturbing. Everyone was sincere and dutiful in what they said, but it seemed a narrow view, a view that looked towards traditional explanations and a sort of jingoistic acceptance. Nobody dared mention words like 'unnecessary' or 'futile' or 'mistake.' There was a grim, unquestioning certainty about it all.

Of course, we will never understand the tragic course of history. It is full of wars, purges, pogroms, gulags and concentration camps. The suffering is, and always has been, totally beyond comprehension. They were all unimaginable human tragedies, not intellectual conundrums to be toyed with, and to look at them in any other way would be to diminish them. In fact anything one said would diminish them. It would be the mistake of the intellect again, just words getting in the way of understanding, abstract ideas substituted for humanity, comparing Beethoven's Ninth Symphony with the scientist's silly transcription. My feeble attempts to understand these things did not imply indifference or coldness, or a morbid curiosity. I *was* bothered about them, and as an engineer with a large streak of inquisitiveness I wanted to unravel them, to discover some sort of explanation for the events in this short and sometimes brutish life of ours. I knew I'd ultimately fail, but that should not stop me trying.

But in a sense any attempt to understand or explain things results in a simplification. Scientists studying the theory of the big bang manage to reduce cosmic events to mathematical formulae on sheets of paper. Those mysterious inky scribbles somehow represent an explosion of such a cataclysmic magnitude that it is utterly beyond our imagination.

Is it possible to understand world history, wars, in terms of collective karma? I have always thought that wars were a far greater tragedy than, say, famines, diseases or natural disasters, for the simple reason that wars are intentional; they could theoretically be avoided. But we don't avoid them. We get enthusiastic, we sing patriotic songs and nominate heroes. Afterwards we become nostalgic. Why, in the middle of the First World War, didn't all the world's leaders simply get together and say to each other, 'Look, this is stupid. It's ridiculous. The suffering is huge, the cost is vast. Let's stop it now and get on with our lives.' But they didn't.

What drove them on? There must have been some sort of imperative, some motivating force that made it all possible. Sri Patanjali's phrase of *Tat sannidhau vairatyagah* tells us that in the vicinity of the settled mind, hostile tendencies disappear. But what if the opposite is also true? In the vicinity of an *unsettled* mind, maybe hostility increases. A person who is highly stressed creates disharmony around him, which in turn gets passed on to others to some degree, like ripples on a pond. If millions of people are all angry the collective desire of a nation may be one of hostility. That hostility may be encapsulated in the persona of the nation's leaders, who make decisions accordingly. All the philosophising, all the supposedly rational arguments, are simply justifications. The monster of human history is born in our collective consciousness.

Supposing, as a thought experiment, we were to take thousands of criminals and instead of locking them up we put them on an island. We say to them, 'You're all free to do what you want, but you cannot leave the island.' We return five years later to see what sort of life they have created for themselves. I suspect we would find a society that represented the collective wishes of its population. There would be persecution and cruelty, suffering and ill-health, and an absence of compassion and justice. That society would be what the criminals in fact wanted, they would have created it, it would be their karma. Even the architecture and environment would be ugly, because it is all an expressed part of the landscape that everyone on the island had collectively created with their thoughts.

It's not too big a leap in our imagination to consider what would happen if these prisoners had access to military weapons. They would probably start a war. They would find some pretext to invade a nearby island. Their leader would be the voice of the people, and everyone would follow eagerly. They would somehow think up a convincing reason to justify the war. If the other island had a similarly stressed population, conflict would almost be inevitable. Throw in a couple of Nazis and you'd have genocide.

But what of the individual caught up in a war? What of a child made to suffer through no fault of their own? Can we explain that in terms of karma?

There comes a point in every investigation, in every theory, where you cannot go any further; it reaches beyond our comprehension. For children to suffer in a war is one of the most heartbreaking and despicable aspects in the history of the human race. The law of karma does not adequately explain it. One could argue that the child had a karmic debt from a previous life, but is nature so callous that it resolves this debt in the life of an infant? A child cannot reflect and cannot learn; it is innocent and helpless. Some eastern thinkers claim that if a person suffers unjustly in one life then nature somehow compensates karmically in the next. I cannot accept that; it suggests that the law is fallible and sometimes breaks down, in which case it is not a law.

Dr Ramana had said that a suffering child offers an opportunity for some people to learn, to value another life, to possibly pay off a karmic debt. But who was learning, and what was the lesson, when children were being shoved into the gas chambers of Auschwitz?

Dear David

I was sorry to hear about your wife's cousin and please accept my condolences. These sad events always provoke reflection alongside the grief but my suggestion is not to discuss matters of karma and such things at this time because people will misunderstand and so may be hurt or offended.

As for the question of karma, is this event the karmic response to an earlier time? Well I am sure it is but nonetheless on an individual level we can never know the exact nature of another's karma as there are so many factors and is thus unknowable and so speculation will be pointless, but we have to come back to the fact that the laws of nature govern these things and we can trust these laws if only we can understand them in just the same way as we trust the law of gravity.

I hope and pray for better future where wars are unnecessary and understanding and tolerance are valued more than military might.

Yours sincerely, K Ramana.

Chapter 18

Averting the Danger to Come

For reasons better left unsaid, Sandy and I decided to go our separate ways. It was a terribly unhappy time for me and for a while I could not accept it; I convinced myself she would come back. I shut myself away and became something of a recluse. I tried to understand the separation in terms of my spiritual growth, my karma, and I re-read a lot of Dr Ramana's letters looking, I suppose, for some kind of solace or explanation. I wrote to Dr Ramana and told him what had happened. I got a letter back a few weeks later from someone claiming to be Dr Ramana's friend. He politely asked me for precise details of when and where I was born. More out of curiosity than hope I sent him the information.

About two weeks later I had a strange but somehow soothing experience. I woke up in the early hours of the morning with the sound of chanting in my ears. It was a dream, but somehow it seemed much more substantial than a dream; it seemed to go around and around in my head. Eventually I went back to sleep. I had a clear recollection of the occurrence the following day and it gave me an inexplicable sense of reassurance. I realised that, although the hurt was still there, a part of me remained untouched, as though I was beyond suffering. It made me think of the time, years ago, when I was in Dr Ramana's hospital and I lay in bed feeling that all was right with the world; everything was in its proper place.

A few days later I received a letter from Dr Ramana. It had been written by somebody else but Dr Ramana had put a small, scrawled signature at the bottom. I have corrected the numerous grammatical and spelling errors.

Dear David

I must apologise for not writing to you before but my health has deteriorated recently, nothing serious but I have one or two diffi-culties. A colleague is writing this on my behalf, but the content is from me. I am so sorry to hear about the sad changes that are taking place in your life. I hope that some of the things we have discussed over the last years will give you a perspective.

I asked for your birth details so that I could get a planetary chart compiled for you by a Jyotishi (often referred to as a Vedic astrologer, though in fact the Vedas say nothing about astrology. The word Jyotish means 'light' or 'illumination'). *Your chart showed clearly that this unfortunate change in your circumstances was inevitable, and this is what you must try to understand; you could not have avoided it. You and your wife were together for a purpose, but now you both have other things to learn as part of your evolution, so your parting is necessary, so all you can do is learn from these times and try to understand more about yourself.*

To a Western mind a jyotish chart may seem difficult to under-stand, but as you know so well now, we each have our individual karma and we are all closely connected to, indeed part of, the universe, so the location of the planets has an intimate connection with us and to our life events, in the same way that a clock has a connection with our day-to-day activities. There is a mathematical harmony between all these things. At certain times your karma must bear fruit and the jyotish chart simply tells us when that will happen.

The timing of the unfoldment of your karma is a critical issue. You may remember the example I once gave you of the poor woman who neglected her children. Well the karmic lessons she will have to learn cannot occur until the circumstances are right. Maybe she needs to love a child before losing it, in order to see things differently and understand the value of human life so a lot of circumstances must first be in place, along with a different mind-set, for that lesson

*to be absorbed because in her present life, with her current mind, she
would never understand it.*

*And it is the same with your unhappy turn of events; they have
occurred now for a reason and they are inevitable, so all you can do
is to try to learn from them, which is why it is happening.*

*I have arranged through a friend to have a yagya performed on
your behalf. A yagya is a Vedic ceremony performed by learned
pundits; they will chant specific Vedic texts along with your name
which will help you through this unfortunate period but it will not
necessarily give you what you wish for because your desires are part
of your ego and the yagya functions on a much subtler, more fundamental level of nature than that, but it will smooth things over,
make things much easier for you. It will help you to discover what
you really need for your evolution and also it will help you to find
yourself.*

Yours sincerely, K Ramana

I was touched by Dr Ramana's concern and intuitively felt that
the experience of three days ago – the night-time chanting–was
the yagya being performed. Knowing this gave me a sense of
reassurance. The chanting had been a tangible event for me; it
gave me a sense of peace and acceptance, and it was reassuring
to know that subtle laws of nature could effortlessly reach out
and have a measurable effect at a distance. Nothing materially
changed in my life, but I felt there was an unmistakable stillness
that seemed to pervade everything I did.

I have to say that the word 'astrology' rang alarm bells with
me. It conjured pictures of strangely-dressed fairground folk
with headscarves and dangling earrings, and a talent for taking
money from gullible passers-by. But the chanting had made me
curious. It was something I had directly experienced; it could not
be ignored.

Dear Dr Ramana

I was sorry to hear that your health has been problematic. I hope you are now fully recovered. Thank you for your letter and thank you also for the yagya that you arranged for me. As a Westerner I must admit this was a novel and intriguing approach to my current personal difficulties, and I have to say is completely outside of my experience. I have been unable so far to gather much information on yagyas and would appreciate any knowledge you have on the subject.

Firstly I must tell you that at some point before I received your letter I had an unusual experience. I awoke in the early hours with the distinct sound of chanting in my ears. It was a tangible experience and I did not dismiss it as being merely a dream. I remembered it clearly the following day. Also tangible was the sense of reassurance that the experience gave me. I am assuming that this was the effect of the yagya.

As I say, this is hugely novel and unconventional to a Westerner. I must admit I would have difficulty accepting it had it not been for the experience of the chanting. As with all of Eastern thought I try to be open minded and I try to understand these matters (as far as one can understand them). I would therefore be grateful for any information on how the yagya is performed, what it consists of and most of all how it works. How, for example, does a yagya create an effect at a distance.

I hope your health continues to improve and I look forward to hearing from you.

With best wishes, David

Dr Ramana replied a few weeks later and I was glad to see that the letter was written in his own hand again, which presumably indicated his return to health.

Dear David

Your question is interesting and has proved to be something of a challenge for me.

How can a yagya exert an influence that averts the danger to come? Why should chanting Vedic texts bring about an effect in 'the world out there'? Orthodox religious folk would claim that a yagya 'pleases the gods' by demonstrating a willingness to make sacrifice of some sort to atone for negative behaviour; but that is a belief, not an understanding and jyotish works on understanding, meaning precise details of place of birth as well as exact time, and allows the pundit to produce enormously intricate birth charts from computer showing position of planets which they interpret, as the pundits are endowed with this knowledge having undergone decades of rigorous training.

The sun, the planets and the moon are regarded as a complex sort of clock comprising numerous hands instead of the normal two and in a sense we can all make predictions in this way because for example I can predict with reasonable certainty that around the time the sun appears on the horizon most people will get out of bed and put on clothes and also when the sun's path dips to its lowest winter point I can predict that millions of people in Christian countries will take their credit card and head for high street for shopping but the planets are not causing this behaviour, they are simply the clock that signals when this behaviour will take place so it is simple mathematics combined with a rudimentary understanding of human behaviour that allows me to make my predictions.

The jyotishis are doing similar thing, but in a far more detailed way so they are able to determine, by reference to a person's birth chart, when certain events are likely to take place. Karmic debts have to be paid off at some point, and lessons must be learned and the jyotishis are able to look at this vast astrological clock and tell us when that lesson is most likely to occur but this is a hugely intricate process, the knowledge of which has been handed down through erudite Brahmin families for countless generations as part of Puranic tradition.

A principal part of jyotish is predicting the onset of karmically *determined events and the destiny we bestowed upon ourselves at an earlier time and the jyotishis are often able to ameliorate the effect of these events by way of yagya* (yajna in Sanskrit) *which is sacrificial fire ceremony that involves numerous pundits chanting ancient Vedic texts. How does this work? How can it cause an effect at a distance?*

Firstly, distance is in itself not an issue because, as we have seen earlier, at the most fundamental levels of nature's functioning, distance – space – is purely a construct of human mind because at quantum level of reality the concept of space ceases to have meaning, so it makes no difference if the yagya is performed in distant land or right next door. Secondly, if our karma is set to come to fruition, surely that is a deterministic event, and so cannot be prevented? But this is like saying that once an arrow has left the bow it is on a prede-termined trajectory and must inevitably reach its destination, but a yagya is like a crosswind; it is a gentle and subtle influence that can affect the ultimate outcome. Jyotish and yagyas are concerned with trends and likelihoods because in fact it often takes only very small factor in our lives to make a huge difference to the direction it takes such as if my car break down I may get the services of a good mechanic to fix it or bad one, in which case I could be in difficulty and also in court case the difference between a good lawyer and an indifferent one can determine result of freedom or life behind bars and these small but valued factors are result of support of nature or absence of it and so have important consequences.

Your letter has made me to consider my understanding of this matter and I have to admit now that I do not fully understand it and how it works in fact only very little of it but I suspect the full and complete understanding can only be conceived when a person fully understands and perceives the unity of all things, that we are all one with the universe and we see that the memory of all events which the universe somehow retains and that the laws of jyotish are like the laws of nature itself which is expressed in mathematics which allows this to happen.

One interesting aspect is that the jyotishis chant your name as a part of the yagya ceremony, which they do to direct the yagya influence to the correct direction, which makes us ask why does your name identify you in this way, which is principle called Nama Rupa which means name and form which means that there is connection at very subtle level of creation between the sound of your name and you as a person, and this connection between name and form is very significant aspect of ancient language of Sanskrit, which is why Vedas are venerated because there is strong connection of name with the form, that is the manifestation in reality of an object or person and the sound or word that identifies it. This is difficult to understand but if you imaginate a large horizontal drum from a music band with a little fine sand spread on surface, then if you lean up close and say aloud a word the drum skin will vibrate which makes sand form into a regular pattern such as circle and in this way can be seen that there is connection between sound you made and the form. This is simplistic illustration of nama rupa, because sound is a vibration and so is everything else in universe so we see there is harmony and connection between the name you have and you as a person so as name is chanted along with Sanskrit texts so the yagya influence is directed to correct place, like an address. So the laws of nature are brought into harmony for that person only, so he will receive full support of nature in everything he endeavours.

But all this is intellectual attempt to understand something when all we need to know is that it in fact works and does produce a predictable change in what we call reality which is itself just sequence of vibrations and I have seen so many times the effect at a distance that you refer so in a sense my understanding is limited but instead I have trust, based on my own experience seeing the effect so many times.

I'm sorry I cannot be more help but I hope this will give you some insight into yagya.

Yours sincerely, K Ramana

It was an interesting reply but it didn't entirely satisfy me. I could understand the point about distance – space – being in a sense irrelevant, but how could the chanting of pundits, however erudite they are, affect the physical circumstances of a person? How could it change reality? The fact that the jyotishis have to undergo years of rigorous training and study to develop this skill means that for me to understand it in any more than a rudimentary way would be impossible. It is like the skill of a surgeon; however hard I try I will never understand what he is doing, but I observe the results and that gives me confirmation that his skills are effective. My experience of the chanting was confirmation of a sort, rather than an explanation, and that should, in a sense, have been sufficient.

But I couldn't let this go; the experience didn't suffice. I needed a solid, rational explanation. Dr Ramana had admitted that his knowledge was limited, so there was no point in asking him. Also, his understanding included the concept of akasha, a sort of nature's memory bank, which I am not entirely comfortable with. The problem seemed to take on an ever greater importance, not just because of the chanting experience, but because of the whole philosophy of karma. It now seemed obvious to me that the force or influence of karma somehow changed the material world to some degree. It has an effect or influence on our lives in a concrete, tangible way. To understand this was, I suppose, fundamental to my understanding of karma.

I started to think about Sandy's cousin Mark, who had died in Iraq. He had apparently been near to a roadside bomb when it exploded and he was killed by flying shrapnel. It could have missed him, indeed it could have gone past just a millimetre away, and his life would have continued for maybe another fifty years, with all that that would entail, such as a family, a career and so on; in fact a totally different history. But that possibility disappeared in an instant, when the shrapnel hit him.

Did Mark make a pre-birth choice to take on a life that would end prematurely, so that he or someone close to him would learn from the experience? Or did the law of karma dictate the outcome of that chance event? If his karma, his thought history, had been different, would the shrapnel not have killed him? Would a yagya have caused the shrapnel to miss him? And if so, how could the yagya have caused that 'effect at a distance'? The only possible explanation I can see, if we disregard the 'hand of God' approach, is that of the 'Many-Worlds Interpretation' of quantum physics and how this relates to the Vedantic description of reality.

I have to hold my hands up and state that my understanding of quantum theory is minimal. But I don't apologise for that, because ignorance in this particular area of knowledge is just a question of degree; nobody fully comprehends it. Richard Feynman, a Nobel Prize winner and one of the most respected scientists in this field, said, 'I think I can safely say that nobody understands quantum mechanics.' And Niels Bohr is quoted as saying: 'Anyone who is not shocked by quantum theory has not understood it.' These difficulties are not entirely matters of IQ points or education; quantum theory is just very difficult to imagine due to its apparent paradoxes, contradictions and absurdities. The world is not only stranger than we think, it's stranger than we *can* think. We in fact have huge limitations when we try to think about things in general, and anyone who tries to tell us that he knows something for certain is deluding himself. Certainty is fine for dictators and religious leaders, but it is a huge impediment if we want to understand the world around us. And nowhere is that more true than in the field of quantum physics.

The nature of the quantum world is unimaginably bizarre. Eleven dimensions of space, parallel universes, bi-location of particles; the idea of karma seems pretty mundane when compared to some of the concepts that scientists ask us to consider. And they are not just speculative theories dreamt up by some slightly batty professor; these ideas have a solid basis in science and mathematics. They cannot be easily dismissed.

Quantum theory proposes that everything is everywhere at once; it has no fixed, concrete existence and is usually defined in terms of probabilities or 'clouds of probabilities.' All of matter is initially expressed in wave form only, the wave being the curve on a graph that indicates the likelihood of a sub atomic particle being in a specific place at a given time. The particle exists in what is called a super-position, because it is above and beyond what we would normally call position, that is, a specific location in time and space.

A part of this theory is referred to as 'Consciousness Causes Collapse.' Consciousness is fundamental to quantum theory and it has puzzled physicists for a long time. Many of them, Wolfgang Pauli and Werner Heisenberg for example, insist that it is an intrinsic and fundamental aspect of this subject, but others disagree; it is still a matter of debate. But according to this theory, once a person's consciousness alights on an object, the wave function 'collapses.' This collapse produces the reality that we see all around us, the hard material objects. Our consciousness is thus an intrinsic part of the reality we live in. It is not a separate process that takes place solely within our brains, as an independent observer. Consciousness causes the collapse, and that collapse creates what we call reality, the world that we all perceive with our senses.

The Many-Worlds Interpretation (MWI) is a specific approach to the understanding of quantum physics. It is not, it must be said, universally accepted, but the majority of physicists regard it as a valid and useful explanation. The idea proposes that, in addition to the world around us that we perceive with our five senses, there are an infinite number of other 'parallel' worlds that we are not aware of. The world we see, our reality, is the 'collapsed' world and the other worlds remain in 'super-position.'

The best way to describe MWI is by way of analogy, although analogies of course always have limits. Imagine I wish to travel in my car to a distant town. I set off, and at the end of my road I turn left. I could have turned right, but I instead I made a conscious decision to turn left. The road to my right clearly exists, and continues to exist, but in my mind it existed only briefly, as a possible option. I am now on the new road and at the end of it is another junction. I make another decision. This process is repeated over and over until I reach my destination. At each and every junction there existed the possibility of another route, another journey, indeed another history, and my choices along the way determined the ultimate outcome.All those other roads could have become a reality, a part of my journey, but at each junction one road became a reality and all the others remained as just possibilities. What became reality and what remained non-reality was decided by my consciousness. (This process does not in fact take place in steps, as the analogy suggests, but is a seamless and fluid progression.)

MWI proposes that at each moment in our lives, at each junction, all possible outcomes are present. But we experience only one of them, the one chosen by our consciousness. And that is what we perceive as reality. The other possible outcomes remain in a super-position; they do not collapse, so do not appear to us as a reality. So there was another world, or indeed worlds, where the piece of shrapnel did not hit Mark and in that world a whole different route map would have unfolded in front of him. But sadly Mark was in the particular world where the shrapnel *did* hit him.

So was it karma that decided which of these numerous worlds Mark was in at that critical instant? This is where quantum theory and Vedanta differ: Vedanta recognises the *quality* of consciousness, not just consciousness itself.

Mark, in that tragic instant, found himself in a world in which the outcome included his demise. He was propelled there by the quality of his own consciousness. The world that he inhabited, and thus the world where he died, had in fact been pre-determined by him. It had been manifested over time by the quality of his consciousness, his thought history, his karma. He had created that world for himself. And it was *that* world, not the others, that took on the property that we call reality.

In the Vedantic world, like the quantum world, there is no distinction made between consciousness and what we call reality, the world outside of ourselves. In his book 'The Hindu Vision,' Alistair Shearer puts it like this: '...the entire universe is alive, structured as an ever-changing field of vibrating energy that is the manifestation of the Supreme Consciousness known as Brahman – the Unbounded.' We continually create our reality with our thoughts, our consciousness. It is all one, and it consists of vibrating energy, a description that is identical to quantum theory's description of reality. Mark's world was an integrated part of that consciousness. In that instant of time, Mark could have stepped forward into any number of worlds, in the same way as my car journey could have taken me left or right, and thus to a different destination. All possibilities existed. In Mark's case his thought history, his karma, determined which specific world would manifest.

Mark's history could have been different; another world could have manifested as his reality. The influence of a yagya, or a different karmic path, could have caused a collapse into a different world, one where he didn't die. But how could that occur? As Dr Ramana said, it often takes only a tiny influence to trigger a major change in circumstances. It stretches the imagination to suppose that the bomb did not explode, or for the shrapnel to fly everywhere but somehow miss Mark, but what if Mark had experienced the thought of moving away from the bomb, just at that critical time? That decision would have been a minute cerebral process, a microscopic event in Mark's brain lasting only milliseconds. Yet it would have changed everything.

And that decision, like the decision to turn left or right at a road junction, would have depended on the quality of Mark's consciousness at that moment.

So could the yagya have changed the outcome? The yagya is chanted; it is sound, it is vibrational. The chanting is in Sanskrit and as Dr Ramana said there is a close relationship between the vibrations of the chanted syllables and the material world that it is a part of. The chanting could have structured Mark's reality, his consciousness, with its vibrations, in the same way as the pattern taken up by a layer of sand sprinkled on a kettle-drum is structured by the sounds that are applied to it. Sounds – vibrations – have an impact on the material world, and there is nowhere that this is more true than at the quantum level of creation. Those sounds would have had a subtle influence on Mark's consciousness. The chanting was not only taking place aurally; it was obviously also a part of the consciousness of the pundits doing the chanting. Our brain is a quantum entity; it is composed of matter made up of unimaginably small quantum particles. And our brain and the world outside of it are totally interconnected at the quantum level; they form an uninterrupted, unified whole. We are in a sense doing our thinking within a boundless, all-encompassing universal field. The pundits are chanting and that harmonious influence imperceptibly permeates our consciousness.

But this is obviously counter-intuitive; surely we think with our brain, which is firmly located within our skull? Dr Moody's description of Near Death Experiences shows this to be untrue, because when we die we carry on thinking. The brain dies, yet our consciousness continues. So the simplistic, mechanical description of thought as an electro-chemical process taking place within our head is incomplete; nature is apparently far more complex than that.

So how does this lead to effects at a distance? The quantum notion of interconnectedness is not an abstract concept used to describe some obscure mathematical equation. It is a real, tangible phenomenon that has been repeatedly proven in the laboratory. In 1935 three scientists, Einstein, Podolsky and Rosen, published a paper which proposed that under given circumstances a particle in one geographical location could instantly influence, indeed physically alter, the motion of a separate particle in another location. The three scientists naturally had difficulty in accepting this idea as it flatly contradicted everything science had taught us so far. Einstein was particularly unhappy as it brought into question the principal tenet of relativity: that nothing can travel faster than light. He later referred to it as 'spooky action at a distance.' Thirty years later another scientist, J S Bell, produced what is known as Bell's Theorem, which confirmed the original paper. Later experiments by Alain Aspect proved this theory beyond all doubt, and it has been replicated many times.

We do our thinking with a brain that is composed of trillions of sub-atomic particles, each of which obeys the laws of quantum physics. These particles really are interconnected, not just with other particles within the brain, but with the entire universe, and thus our thoughts are too. Our own individual consciousness is part of a much bigger whole. The yagya would thus have had an effect on Mark's consciousness, which could have allowed him to create – collapse – a different world out of the super-position. It could do this because, at the quantum level of reality, his consciousness, the jyotishi's consciousness and the totality of consciousness that the Vedas call Brahman, were all one. They were an integrated, inseparable whole. Thus the particular world Mark's consciousness could have chosen may have been one where there was a different outcome, perhaps one where he didn't die.

On the surface level, this different reality would have been seen by Mark and everyone around him as a lucky escape, good fortune or even the grace of God. It would have been nothing of the sort. The events and choices were all triggered by Mark's thought-history, his karma. Before those thoughts collapsed into a particular reality, they could have been modified by the jyotishis, using a subtle but clever manipulation of the laws of nature.

The word 'collapse' is perhaps confusing in this context. In general usage, collapse describes disintegration. If a building collapses, or if a business enterprise collapses, it suggests destruction or failure, resulting in chaos. But the quantum usage of the word suggests just the opposite. It indicates construction, integration or a coming together. To me, a more appropriate word would be 'coalesce,' meaning the joining of disparate components into a unified whole.

We sometimes see a picture of this process in nature. In the county of Somerset, in the UK, there are spectacular displays on spring and autumn evenings involving hundreds of thousands of starlings. These individual birds, as they flock together, create an almost solid display of swirling patterns in the sky, which is a useful picture of how particles combine. The birds each arrive from different locations and they coalesce into a shape. In a sense this is what physical matter does; trillions of particles collectively coalesce to create the illusion of solid matter when we observe it.

But, to continue the analogy, our senses do more than just observe; the pattern that emerges relies for its very existence on our consciousness as the observer. Imagine for a moment that some people are watching the activities of these birds. Then try to imagine that these people could unwittingly influence the patterns or shapes to be created, by the quality of their thoughts. One could quite easily see that an angry person may create a shape of something associated with anger, such as a gun; a depressed person might create a pattern like a black cloud and a placid individual may produce a beautiful waterfall. Each observer would create a reality, a world, according to the quality of his own consciousness, all from the same disparate components. Consciousness creates our world, our circumstances, and it creates the route that we take on our own individual journey.

This is why meditation is so vitally important. It raises our level of consciousness. It purifies the individual's nervous system, effectively burning up the seeds of karma and allows a person to create a reality that is free of suffering.

I had by now read about half a dozen books on particle physics. My head was spinning. Niels Bohr had a point when he said that we should be shocked by quantum theory; after every chapter I had to have a cup of tea and a sit down. In the end I despaired of achieving anything more than a rudimentary knowledge, so I put the books to one side. I reminded myself that I was trying to understand karma, not science. I began to suspect I was falling into good old Wittgenstein's trap of over-intellectualising everything, and the Sanskrit phrase of Pragya Parad came to mind, 'the mistake of the intellect.' I was confusing the map with the territory.

I was by now comfortable with the laws of karma. My understanding of it was far from complete, but that is true of any subject. As Karl Popper said, all theories are to some extent provisional. I had learned enough from Dr Ramana and from my own investigations and experiences to convince me that karma is a real and tangible phenomenon, and that it is an important influence on the lives of each and every one of us. Hopefully my knowledge would continue to grow. I would endeavour to keep an open mind, and to always discriminate, dissect and reason.

But maybe these intentions were to some extent superfluous; it would be the quality of my consciousness that allowed the unfoldment of my understanding, not learning from a book. So all I needed to do was to meditate.

Another minor change took place, which gave me a sense of optimism. I had always watched TV programmes about the two world wars with a mixture of curiosity, disgust, and bewilderment. Why, I would ask myself, does the human race continue in this way? I would watch a documentary about Poland, surely the most tragic of nations, and ask myself why there was no explanation, or indeed any attempt at an explanation, for the events that had occurred there. But now my admittedly simplistic and incomplete concept of karma gave me a hint of a way forward in my understanding; I could look at broadcasts about conflict and tragedy in a subtly different way.

Europe, indeed much of the world, had been populated at that time by millions of people who, like Mark, were creating their own reality. Each one of them was, with their own consciousness and through the medium of the collective consciousness, unwittingly generating a world full of fear, hatred and intolerance. The outcome, that is the destruction and suffering, was inevitable given the collective thought-history of the population. It wasn't a series of accidents; it wasn't simply poor decision-making by incompetent politicians. We created it. We created it with our consciousness.

If we could fully understand this, and if we could use that understanding to our advantage, there could genuinely be peace in our time.

Chapter 19

The Last Lesson

Now I was on my own I began to take meditation much more seriously. Months slowly passed, then years, and the pain of my marriage break-up began to subside. I developed a cautious optimism. I focussed on inner fulfilment, as opposed to outward pleasures, and I eventually found myself with a tenuous yet delicious sense of independence. I could do what I wanted and go where I pleased. I had no obligations, no responsibilities and a bit of money in the bank. I did a couple of longish meditation courses and seriously considered becoming a yoga teacher. But all of that could wait; right now there were places to see and things to do. It was a time pregnant with possibilities, and I set off with a growing determination to enjoy my freedom.

I decided I'd first go back to India and visit Dr Ramana. Then I would travel to the Himalayas, go to a couple of ashrams and take the tourist route. I smiled at the thought of it. I grew more enthusiastic by the day and wrote to tell the learned doctor of my plans.

I arrived at Delhi airport at two in the morning. Even at that hour it buzzed with activity and I was besieged by taxi drivers and hawkers. It was hot, humid and smelled of aviation fuel. I was tired and a bit impatient with the crowds of people. A driver met me and as we walked to his car the heat hit me like a wall. We set off into traffic thick with exhaust fumes. We joined a queue and eventually passed two smashed-up cars and a bullock cart. A man lay on the ground encircled by a handful of gesticulating people.

I was soon in my hotel room having a shower. I slept late the next day, then sat and stared lazily out of the eighth floor window. I thought of my last visit to India over 20 years ago and

I suddenly missed being with Sandy. I felt lost and alone, with vivid, aching memories of her and the optimism we had once shared. After breakfast I did a short meditation and slept again for an hour, then had a swim in the deserted, sky-blue pool.

I had to take a train to the district where the hospital was located. I knew Dr Ramana lived within walking distance of his workplace. It would be easy to find him; he had worked at the hospital for decades so somebody would know him.

New Delhi railway station was busy and I looked around at the multitude of people. I had never seen such crowds. Everyone was hurrying; everyone was carrying something. There was a smell of traffic fumes, tea and incense. A beggar propped up against a wall, his gnarled arm prominent, contrasted with the pretty black-haired girls in bright saris. Children tried to sell me trinkets: plastic Taj Mahals painted a cheap gold and gaudy pictures of Hindu saints. Others simply grinned mischievously and held out their hands. The char-wallah shouted to me, laughed and raised a brown earthenware teacup. A train arrived and a sea of passengers swept across the platform. I took refuge in the booking hall. I bought a ticket, turned away and merged into the moving crowd. I put the ticket into my wallet and looked around for the platform number.

Suddenly Dr Ramana was before me, smiling warmly. I stared at him, dumbfounded. How did he know I'd be here? For a second or two I couldn't speak.

"David! I'm so glad you came," he exclaimed. He looked at me intently, then laughed. "It is simple. Everything is so simple: just be kind to people. That is all. That is everything. Be kind."

With that he turned and hurried away.

I still hadn't uttered a word. I grabbed my bag and raced after him, but he had disappeared into the crowd. I paced up and down for a few minutes, then stood on some steps and looked around. I couldn't see him anywhere. Everything seemed to be quiet and distant. I watched the hoards of people and spontaneously sensed I was a part of them, as if they were my family, as if I belonged here, with them. I suddenly felt tearful and in awe of this struggling mass of humanity, each laden with cares and hopes, each striving unknowingly towards love. Be kind, Dr Ramana had said.

I got onto my train and sat down, perplexed. Was I dreaming? Why did he hurry away? Why was I feeling like this? I watched people streaming through the carriage, hoping I might see the learned doctor. I peered out of the window. As the train slowly started to move I began to doubt if I had actually seen him, as he had looked far younger than I would have imagined after 20 years. But it *was* him; the mannerisms, the appearance. There could be no doubt about it. And after all, he had clearly recognised me and used my name. I couldn't have been mistaken.

I left the train a few stops later and asked for directions to the hospital. Everything seemed different. I'd had a picture in my head of the surrounding district but it had all changed. There were now lots of trees, and the once deserted street was full of people, hooting cars and ringing bicycles. A camel was tethered to some railings; an old man in a turban chewed thoughtfully on a cheroot as he watched the traffic.

I soon found the hospital. It looked worn and grey, and there was a collection of food and drink stalls clustered around the entrance. I entered and approached the reception desk. I didn't recognise anything; my memory must have misled me. The waiting area was full of patients and children, each in need of care. I watched as a dog wandered in, glanced around, then trotted out. It gave me a suspicious, sidelong glance.

I explained to one of the receptionists that I was a friend of Dr Ramana's, that I knew he was now retired, and asked if she could give me his address. She was polite and helpful. She remembered Dr Ramana from a long time ago and knew somebody, another doctor, who was a friend of his. She spoke briefly on the telephone and turned back to me. "Somebody is coming to see you."

I sat and waited. About twenty minutes later a middle-aged lady approached. She was well dressed and had pure white hair. A stethoscope hung around her neck. I stood up as she took off her glasses and introduced herself.

"I am Dr Devata," she said. "I was friend of Dr Ramana."

I explained the purpose of my visit. I mentioned our lengthy correspondence and she nodded, as if she knew of it. I told her I had just seen Dr Ramana briefly at New Delhi railway station but had lost him in the crowd.

She gently took my hand. "David," she said, looking intently at me. "That is not possible. Dr Ramana died just over a week ago."

I stared at her. This didn't make sense. "But I saw him," I said. "An hour ago. He spoke to me... he used my name."

"David, I am telling you truth. I'm sorry. I was with him when he died. I attended his cremation."

A few days later I stepped off a bus in Himachal, high in the Himalayas. I checked in to a small hotel and had a late lunch. I lay on my bed in the afternoon, exhausted after the tortuous bus journey along precipitous mountain roads. I thought of Sandy again, wondered what she was doing, then reflected on my encounter with Dr Ramana. Be kind, he'd said. The words appeared spontaneously in my mind, like a softly whispered echo. I felt overwhelmed by an enormous gratitude towards him, for all he had taught me, and for the utter simplicity of his final lesson.

Later that day I took a taxi to a beauty spot about twenty minutes distant. I paid the driver and told him I would walk back to town. He gave me a curious look, pocketed my hefty tip and drove off. I watched as the car made its dusty way down the dusty hill towards the dusty town, far in the distance. The sound of the motor grew ever fainter, until there was silence.

I looked around, then climbed up the slope and away from

the road. I walked steadily for an hour, sometimes amongst trees, sometimes scrambling over rocks. I turned and looked back. The scenery was spectacular; I had never seen anything like it. I saw snow-capped peaks in the distance, beneath a diamond-blue sky. I saw waterfalls, fir forests and soaring birds, and the twisty, uneven road ahead of me. There was an astounding clarity and purity about everything, and a deep, reverberating stillness. I felt exhilarated by the beauty of it all, and of my tiny place within it.

I sat quietly for an hour, perched on a rock. As the sky slowly darkened stars appeared everywhere, thousands of them. I watched, enchanted, as Venus appeared over the edge of the world and began to spread its gentle light. I didn't think about anything. I didn't reflect on how I had arrived at this place or where I would go next. I simply luxuriated in the moment. And the silence.

Bibliography

Moody, Dr Raymond. *Life After Life* Harper Collins ISBN 0-06-251739-2

Newton, Dr Michael, *Journey of Souls* Llewellyn ISBN 978-1-56718-485-3

Shearer, Alistair *The Hindu Vision* Thames & Hudson ISBN 0-500-81043-5

Stevenson, Dr Ian *Birthmarks & Birth Defects Corresponding to Wounds on Deceased Persons* (Paper – June 1992) University of Virginia School of Medicine, USA

Weiss, Dr Brian, *Many Lives, Many Masters* Piatkus ISBN 0-7499-1378-9

Further Reading

Armstrong, Karen *Buddha* Phoenix ISBN 978-0-7538-1340-9

Capra, Fritjof *The Tao of Physics* Flamingo ISBN 0-00-654489-4

Fenwick, Dr Peter & Elizabeth *The Truth in the Light* Headline ISBN 0-7472-1186-8

Newton, Dr Michael, *Destiny of Souls* Llewellyn ISBN 978-1-56718-499-0

Rama, Swami *Living with the Himalayan Masters* Himalayan Institute Press ISBN 978-0-89389-156-5

Rinpoche, Sogyal. *The Tibetan Book of Living & Dying* Rider ISBN 0-7126-7139-0

Russell, Peter *The TM Technique* (Meditation) Arkana ISBN 0-14-019229-8

Shearer, Alistair *Buddha – The Intelligent Heart* Thames & Hudson ISBN 0-500-81038-9

Shearer, Alistair *Effortless Being - The Yoga Sutras of Patanjali* Mandala ISBN 0-04-440520-0

Weiss, Dr Brian *Through Time Into Healing* Piatkus ISBN 0-7499-1835-7

BOOKS

Iff Books is interested in ideas and reasoning. It publishes material on science, philosophy and law. Iff Books aims to work with authors and titles that augment our understanding of the human condition, society and civilisation, and the world or universe in which we live.